"FORE" Open-Minded Birkdale Boys

The story of Alfie Fyles & his caddy colleagues

Mags Eatock & John Murray

"FORE" Open-Minded Birkdale Boys
The story of Alfie Fyles & his caddy colleagues

Mags Eatock & John Murray

ISBN: 978-0-9955818-1-4

This book is produced by Mags Eatock & John Murray Publishing in conjunction with **WRITERSWORLD**, and is produced entirely in the UK. It is available to order from most bookshops in the United Kingdom, and is also globally available via UK based Internet book retailers.

WRITERSWORLD
2 Bear Close Flats, Bear Close, Woodstock
Oxfordshire, OX20 1JX, England
☎ 01993 812500
☎ +44 1993 812500

www.writersworld.co.uk

The text pages of this book are produced via an independent certification process that ensures the trees from which the paper is produced come from well managed sources that exclude the risk of using illegally logged timber while leaving options to use post-consumer recycled paper as well.

Brother and sister John Murray and Mags Eatock were raised in the Marshside area of Southport in a poor but strong family unit. Being born during the late forties and early fifties respectively, they experienced post-war conditions, the teddy boy era, the affluent and rapidly changing sixties etc. etc.

John loved sports from an early age and Mags enjoyed all aspects of the arts. John was captain of the Park Golf Club in 2009 and was proud to be elected again in the centenary year of 2014. He has built up successful roofing and pitch & putt businesses, whilst Mags has been a teacher/artist and is now a Reiki Master.

John and Alfie Fyles had a very special relationship - Alf was a 'good friend and drinking partner' (John's words). He also took John under his wing, becoming an influential avuncular figure. Long before John met and subsequently married Alfie's niece Debbie, Alfie and John regularly caddied in the competitions held at local golf clubs such as Royal Birkdale, Southport and Ainsdale, Hillside, and the Hesketh.

Alf was a very personable and charming man who had amassed a wealth of stories and anecdotes which would keep people laughing for hours, but only his nearest and dearest saw the pain he often experienced in his life. In 1994, when Alf was on his death bed, John asked him if he had any regrets in life and he said just two - the first, that he and Pat, the love of his life, his wife and mother of his children, had become estranged, and the second, that he had never fulfilled his dream to write and publish his life-story.

The idea nagged at John, and a few years later he approached Mags to write Alf's biography. Due to their own mother's illness and subsequent death, the idea went on the back burner for a number of years but was regenerated in 2014: this book is the result.

Most of the information and anecdotes for this book were gathered from Alfie and his colleagues as they regaled people with their many stories. We should therefore like to thank all the family, friends, colleagues and confidantes of the characters mentioned in this book for the wealth of material which they afforded us, as well as express our appreciation of the following websites. (For the sake of accuracy and clarity we have researched the more technical aspects of their tales and some stories have been dramatized to maintain the integrity of the book.)

Bill Fields:
www.golfdigest.com/story/gw20080711fields

Lewine Mair:
www.telegraph.co.uk/sport/golf/theopen/5778997/The-Open-greatest-moments-duel-in-the-sun-Turnberry-1977.html

Tony Manfred:
http://www.businessinsider.com/wartime-golf-rules-2012-2?IR=T

www.bbc.co.uk/programmes/b0645bj1

www.englandsgolfcoast.com/courses

https://garyplayer.com/the-player-foundation/our-story/

www.golf.com/tour-and-news/hitler-invitational-inside-adolf-hitlers-1936-golf-tournament

www.golfsouthport.co.uk/index.html

www.hillside-golfclub.co.uk

www.peteralliss.co.uk

http://www.therichmondgolfclub.com/wartime-rules/

www.royalbirkdale.com/club-history

www.sandagolfclub.co.uk/the-club/club-history

www.sefton.gov.uk/sport-leisure/golf-in-sefton/southport-golf-links.aspx

www.southportvisiter.co.uk/news/nostalgia-more-local-casualties-war-11567643

www.thoughtco.com/the-british-open-1564543

www.thoughtco.com/british-open-winners-1561074

https://en.wikipedia.org/wiki/1967_Piccadilly_World_Match_Play_Championship

https://en.wikipedia.org/wiki/Alcan_Open

https://en.wikipedia.org/wiki/Southport

Chapters

Introduction

Some of the terms within the book

bagging: Where a non-professional caddy without knowledge of the course carries a golfer's bag of clubs.

caddying: Where a professional or knowledgeable caddy is hired to carry a golfer's bag and clubs around the course, often advising them on the best club to use in the circumstances and offering insightful information and moral support.
The Scottish word "caddie" is believed to have been borrowed from the French when military cadets carried golf clubs for royalty.

DA: Term use in the late '50s for a hair style in which a man would sculpt the back of his hair into a quiff resembling a duck's tail (more commonly known as a 'duck's arse'!).

gobbler: Slang term for a long distance, hard-hit putt that holes out (goes into the hole).

gollying: Intentionally walking part of the golf course to find balls that have been lost in play by previous players. Many locals would do this to make pin money - selling the balls back to the golfers or selling them on to local sports shops.

halve the match: At the end of play both players end up all square (also called an honourable half)

'man': The colloquial name for the golfer the caddy is paired up with.

Mrs Greenleaves: Alf and his colleagues would often sleep rough when they did not have money for accommodation at competitions and this was his reference to sleeping under bushes, trees etc.

Open: All references to the Open refer to the British Open unless otherwise stated.

par: This indicates the standard to which golfers aspire i.e. the number of strokes it typically takes an expert golfer to move the ball from the tee until it ends up in the hole.

pot of scouse: A local dish similar to stew or hotpot. It was a cheap, nutritious meal and would have been eaten a few times a week. Often a large pan would be made at the beginning of the week - some families would reheat the meal each day until it was all gone.

pro: Professional golfer

pro-am: Where a professional golfer is paired up with an amateur (often a celebrity)

putt: To hit the ball gently with a putter so that it rolls along the green and into the hole.

yardages: Alf would work out the distance to the hole, considering any hazards, weather conditions etc. so that he could advise the golfer on the best club to use. He was one of the first caddies to start using yardages regularly. Alf would refer to his self-created book containing images of all the courses he had worked on; he would change his recommendations on a daily basis depending on the wind/rain/humidity and so on as these could all affect the outcomes of the shot.

Who's Who

Edward (Teddy or Ted) Fyles: May 20, 1898, to December 9, 1991

Ted Fyles worked at Birkdale golf course from the age of 14 until he was nearly 90. Generally referred to in the book as Ted so as to distinguish him from Teddy Halsall. Father of eight children including Alf and Albert, two of the Birkdale Four. Between the four of them they won many other major tournaments as well as the ones listed below.

Alfie Fyles: November 10, 1926, to March 17, 1994
Caddied for -
Gary Player: won 3 World Match Plays; 2 runners up; 1 British Open Championship
Gay Brewer: won Alcan Open 1967 and 1968
Tom Watson: won 5 British Open Championships in 1975; 1977; 1980; 1982 and 1983

Albert Fyles: 1937 to July 7, 2007
Caddied for -
Tom Weiskopf: Piccadilly World Match Play 1972; 1973 British Open Championship
Tom Kite: 4 major tournaments

Bobby (Jackie) Leigh: 1939 to March 3, 2004
Caddied for -
Peter Thomson: 1965 British Open Championship
Greg Norman: 1980 Suntory World Match Play

Teddy Halsall: 1937 to December 15, 2005
Caddied for -
Billy Casper
Johnnie Miller: 1976 British Open Championship 1937

Introduction

On July 30th, 1889, a group of gentlemen sat in the parlour at No. 23 Weld Road in the north-west town of Southport, England, chatting about their passion for golfing. They made a decision that would impact on the sporting fraternity for many years. Messrs J C Barrett, George Crowther, R L Worsley, Digby Johnson, John Coney, R G Hayward, W M Simpson, B R Simpson, and W W P Shatwell came to an agreement that they would form a golf club, which would be named Birkdale.

Local land owner, Mr Weld Blundell, offered ground in Liverpool Road for an annual rent of £5, and in return was invited to become the first president of the club. The club was duly opened on October 5th with Mr R G Hayward becoming the first captain. In the December of that year, members voted in favour of allowing ladies to use the links (although not on a Saturday or Bank Holiday and not exceeding three days per week!) The first ladies were elected in 1890, and the ladies' section has been an integral and important part of the club ever since.

The original nine-hole course was built on Shaw Hills, behind Bedford Road, on the site that is now Bedford Park, and in 1897 it was moved to its current site in Birkdale Hills, where an eighteen-hole course was constructed.

On May 20th 1898, baby Edward Fyles came into the world. He would make an impact of his own, and, albeit a lesser impact than the opening of the club, it was nonetheless a significant one.

1

March 1912 - Start of an Era

Teddy slowly roused, gathering his thoughts and trying desperately to restart the dream he had been having. In his dream he had money beyond comprehension, and he was sitting in front of a roaring fire in the hearth of the great hall in his mansion house. On the walls hung silky tapestries and magnificent oil paintings. Next to him sat a beautiful lady, her face partially obscured by the firelight shadows.

As he stirred, in the first few seconds of waking he thought the dream was real, but as the images of rich tapestries, the lady and the fire faded, he opened his eyes to see bare walls and the snuffed-out candle at the side of the bed, and realised he was at home.

The warmth of the bed was comforting in stark contrast with the cold of the room, and he groaned as he noticed the delicate patterns etched in frost on the window. His breath hung in the air as he yawned and stretched, then turned over to face his younger brother's tousled hair and pale complexion. His brother smiled enigmatically and Teddy wondered what *he* was dreaming about. He lay for a few more moments while the last vestiges of sleep dissipated, then remembered the task ahead of him.

Quickly and without thinking of the cold linoleum under his warm feet, he leapt from the bed and started to dress. There would be time enough to wash when he got back. The kitchen would be freezing and the house too cold to stay undressed for any length of time. Fuel for the fire was expensive and scarce, so although his mother would make the fire in an hour or so, it was only if they had enough coal and wood that day. Ted planned to go to the shore later. Coal was regularly washed up on to the sand and he could easily bring home a couple of scuttles-full. He would stay out picking until his freezing hands and feet made him return, or until dusk, whichever happened first. He would then bring it home in the old pram his mother had bought off a neighbour many years ago, just after he had been born. One of the wheels was a bit buckled but it served its purpose, and providing he didn't pick up any pieces containing gas, they could have a brilliant fire later that evening. Coal containing gasses banged and spat out burning sparks onto the floor and on to anyone who had the misfortune to be sitting too close to the fire at the time. This had happened to him as a small child and now he was careful to make sure he didn't pick up any. Sometimes, though, it was hidden inside a lump of coal, so you couldn't always tell.

Teddy guessed it was around 5.30 a.m. He could hear his mother in the kitchen and his heart lurched at the thought of her getting up an hour earlier than everyone else to prepare for the day. He could hear his father in the front bedroom snoring gently, not needing to get up for hours and oblivious to the activity in the rest of the house, or the frost that chilled the air. He pulled on his thin, worn trousers and dressed in the jumper with the hole in the elbows - lovingly darned, until it was almost more darn than knitting. He found a pair of thick woollen socks which had been a present on his last birthday and pulled them up, tucking a frayed trouser leg into the top of each one. He crept out of the bedroom and eased himself down the bare wooden stairs, avoiding the ones that creaked so as not to wake anyone.

"Morning, Mam," he said, putting his hand on her shoulder and kissing her softly on the cheek. "Any bread this morning?"

"Aye, lad, I've got it ready in the larder and there's some butter to top it as well."

"*One for you, one for me and one for the pot,*" she quoted as she put three teaspoons of tea into the teapot and filled it with the boiling water from the huge kettle which bubbled on the stove. She always quoted that rhyme - he couldn't imagine a cup of tea without it. He took hold of the cup and warmed his hands around it, not caring that there was no milk to lighten it. As he bit into the doorstep of bread and thinly spread, but delicious, salty butter, he looked furtively at his mother's back and heaped three spoonfuls of sugar into the cup. He jumped as she chided him.

"Teddy Fyles, I've got eyes in the back of my head and I can see you with that sugar. You know we must be careful. I can't afford to get any more this week and if your dad can't sweeten his tea there'll be hell to pay."

"Sorry, Mam."

But she smiled as she walked up behind him, ruffling his hair and pretending to be cross. *God knows, he's a good lad and he does anything he can to help out*, she thought, and her heart melted as she looked at his worn-out shoes, pants and coat, which would afford little protection against the cold on that bitter March day.

"For goodness sake, Teddy, don't forget your scarf and hat. It's freezing today and you'll catch your death on that golf course if you're not careful."

Another quick peck on the cheek and fourteen-year-old Teddy was out the door, gasping as the biting wind turned his breath to icy particles which sparkled in the air as he emerged from the house. It was just after the turn of the 20th century and what was to happen in the next few hours would impact the lives of four boys who would not be born for another decade, plus many professional golfers who were either not yet born or were too young to appreciate the game.

Teddy made his way to Birkdale golf course a mile away and stepped through the gap in the hedge, looking left and right as he zigzagged his way over to the rough on the fourth hole. Slowly, gently, he trod down in and around the scrub. His feet were well sensitised to the feel of a misplaced ball - he had been roaming this course and that of the recently built Hillside and Southport &

Ainsdale (S&A) clubs with his father for years. He took off a glove and bent down to pick up the first round white treasure he had been seeking. He turned it over in his hand looking for cuts or gouges in the coating. By finding the lost balls, cleaning them up and selling them back to club members, he could increase the family coffers by a few pennies a week.

"This could bring me a few coppers," he mumbled to himself as he rolled the ball around his palm. "Bit of a scrub and Mr J will pay me a farthing at least."

On he went, collecting balls as he walked, humming to himself and thinking of his mother's words. She had been telling him she had eyes in the back of her head for as long as he could remember. When he was small, he used to brush her hair for her, secretly looking for the eyes underneath her thick, silky, flame-coloured mane, and he was always mystified not to find them.

"Eyes in the back of her head!" He chuckled as he picked up another ball and put it in his pocket. Becoming aware of a dog barking in the distance, he stopped and craned his head. Something didn't feel right, but he simply assumed someone was taking their pet for an early morning walk.

"Must be mad," he muttered. "If Mam didn't need the money I'd still be enjoying my sleep. God only knows why anyone would get up this early if they didn't need to."

Absent-mindedly he ploughed on, the cold numbing his barely covered fingers and slowing his functions, which forced him to ignore the warning signs that might ordinarily have made him give up and go home. Many golfers were early risers and it didn't do to let people see you 'gollying'. Some members were to be trusted and welcomed the chance to buy good balls at a fraction of the price of new ones, but some would shop you in as soon as look at you. He remembered one punter ranting and raging about him trying to sell back the balls he had found and he had been careful to steer away from that gent ever afterward.

As he moved forward he became aware that the dog had stopped barking, leaving an eerie silence, although he thought he had heard whispers from the copse of woods to his left. He stood still for a couple of minutes, straining to pick up on any further voices. No noise came so he carried on, more cautiously this time, until a voice behind startled him and made him jump.

"I've got you this time, my boy."

John Gillan, the head green keeper, and his yappy terrier stared out from the trees, with one of the junior keepers grinning inanely behind them. This was a rat-faced, spotty boy about two years older than himself and Teddy recognised him from somewhere. He thought it might have been from the village or maybe from his school days. The kid laughed a cruel sneering laugh and in that instance Teddy hated him more than he had hated anyone he ever knew.

"Follow me," the green keeper ordered, and Teddy did so because he had no other option.

The boy walked behind him, occasionally prodding him in the back and making snide remarks. "You realise you could go to jail for this, don't you? That's stealing, that is. I bet your mother and father will be disgusted. I never stole a thing in my life. Thief!"

Teddy was angry, ashamed and scared. He knew what could happen to him and it was not only the freezing weather that caused him to shiver. The dog ran around his ankles growling and snarling as they walked. He wasn't afraid of dogs, and would have kicked out to ward the animal off, but he daren't do so in these circumstances. He was in enough trouble already, so he endured this further ignominy as the solemn procession made its way to the club house.

He couldn't imagine going to jail. He had heard many, many horror stories of what happened to people in custody, and he followed the green keeper numbly as they entered the building and then into his office.

Teddy was told to sit in the corner of the room and the older boy was discharged with whispered instructions. He smirked at Teddy as he passed him, exuding a self-important superiority that made Teddy shrink back into the uncomfortable, hard chair he was sitting on. The green keeper sat behind his huge oak desk and started writing his report. Every minute felt like a lifetime and every so often he fired a question at Teddy, repeating the answer as he wrote.

"Fyles. Edward."

"It's Teddy …"

But the man wasn't listening and continued, "Fourteen years of age. Address, Fyles?"

He stopped abruptly as the door opened and an imposing figure walked into the room accompanied by the rat-faced kid who had been sent to find him. The green keeper stood up sharply and addressed the captain of the golf club.

"Good morning, sir, I have been preparing my report. I have the offender here, sir, and I feel we have a good case for prosecution." His staccato voice stabbed at Teddy's brain, every pointed syllable further depleting his confidence. By the time he was ordered to stand on the carpet in front of the desk, he regretted having eaten the bread and butter that morning as he thought he was going to be sick.

The captain looked at him over half-moon glasses.

"Well ..." He paused and looked at the green keeper's report. "Fyles, what have you got to say for yourself?"

Teddy stood erect. He wouldn't kowtow. He wouldn't crawl or whimper. He was a proud boy from a proud family and he had been taught it was best to get into trouble honestly rather than lie or give feeble excuses. He tried to talk, but his mouth was so dry he could only whisper.

"Speak up, boy. You have committed a crime here, you know. 'Keeping by finding' is still stealing and is a serious offence. What is it? Women? Alcohol? Are you gambling the money you so erroneously earn from the sale of these illegally procured balls? Talk to me or I will call for the constabulary right now."

Teddy pulled himself up to his fullest height.

"No, sir," he said. "It's for me mam. We're a big family and she can't afford to keep us all. Me dad's not working right now and the little ones don't have warm clothes or enough food to eat every day. I'm truly sorry, but I can't think of any other way to help the family out - there's no jobs going anywhere. I've looked and looked and I just need to help her, sir."

Teddy was aware of a tear welling up in the corner of his eyes. Blast! He hadn't wanted that to happen. It was the first time he had spoken about their predicament and he hadn't realised how worried he was. He forced his emotions back down and took a deep breath as he continued. "I can't go to jail, sir, they need me. Me mam gets up dead early to get the kids ready and I don't know how they will manage if ..." His voice broke and he turned his face downwards as he stopped talking, not wanting the rat-faced boy to see him cry.

He remained looking at the floor.

Fighting back the tears, he didn't see the captain's eyes mist over or notice as he took the carefully laundered handkerchief from his pocket to blow his nose. The captain gulped and paused for a long minute, his own thoughts miles away as he regained his composure.

Teddy forced his own thoughts back into the room. He wouldn't think about his mother's drawn face or how she might wring her hands in the courtroom as he was led away to the cells when he was sentenced. Silently he admonished himself and took a few breaths before looking up again. Rat face was relishing his plight, sitting slouched in an easy chair over by the huge bay window, arms folded as he considered his shiny black boots, waiting for the captain's axe to fall.

The captain gestured to the green keeper to follow him into an anti-room and they seemed to take hours, their voices rising and falling in heated debate. Finally, they emerged with grave faces and Teddy could feel the cold steel of the handcuffs around his wrists. Fear crept up from his feet and settled somewhere around his belly. He felt himself flush as the captain motioned for him to come forward.

"Well, Fyles, we have discussed this situation at length and we have come to a decision which we hope we will not live to regret. You seem like a decent lad and you also seem to need a regular wage. We appreciate your predicament and," he paused, and in those few seconds Teddy experienced a hundred different emotions, "we have a scheme here at Birkdale which employs boys as caddies - we also have a vacancy for a gentleman's cloakroom attendant and we wondered if you would like to take up the position. It would supplement your family's income. There is also a social aspect to working here which you could participate in. It is not free and you would be expected to pay a joining fee of one penny, then the same amount would be paid weekly towards the running of the Boys' club at 51 Brighton Road. You would also have to pay for your uniform, but the scheme seems to work well for all our other boy caddies."

Teddy's head spun. He could hear the captain talking about how he expected loyalty, honesty etc. etc., but he didn't take in any of it. A few minutes before, he had been facing a jail sentence, and now he was being offered a job which would boost the family's income no end. The captain gave him a time to report in on the following Monday morning and he just about registered what he was saying.

"Well, son, what do you say?"

"Thank you very much, sir, I'll see you on Monday at seven o'clock, sir." And with that he went outside, threw up and ran all the way home to tell his mother. She was in the front room, darning a much-worn pair of trousers as he knelt in front of her. Her reaction was one which he would remember all his life. At first she thought he was joking and leaned over to gently push his shoulder, telling him not to mess with her. Realising he was serious, disbelief soon turned to amazement followed by delight as the implications dawned on her. After hugging him she excused herself, disappearing into the kitchen on the pretext of making a cup of tea. When out of sight she began to cry silently, looking upwards and mouthing, "Thank you, Lord, thank you so very much."

Teddy reported for duty on the Monday morning and it was the start of a working relationship which would last 74 years, with Teddy remaining in the same humble position, carrying out various duties until 1987 when he was nearly ninety years of age. He was paid one shilling and sixpence a week for his cloakroom duties, which was one of the lowest wages at the club. However, most of the members would give him a few pennies extra for cleaning their clubs and shoes when they returned to the club house, which made the job far more lucrative. He also made a little extra by caddying on his days off.

Teddy made some close friends at the club, including the rat-faced boy David who, once you got to know him wasn't that bad, and Thomas, who started work a few weeks after Teddy. He gave his mother most of his wages, which meant there was now some regular income to feed and clothe them and provide the occasional luxury, and his father could return to enjoying his daily newspaper, something that had been denied him since he lost his job the previous year.

When World War 1 was declared in September 1914, Ted wanted to enlist but, at sixteen he was too young, as men could not join up until they were eighteen. Ironically, he would be too old to enlist for World War 2 - a point that was always a bone of contention for him as he bitterly wanted to do his duty. Continuing to work at the club, Ted saw many of his family and friends go to war, never to return. Many of the big tournaments, including the British Open, which was first played at Prestwick in 1860, were not played between 1915 and 1919.

2

Post-World War 1

After the war ended Britain returned to a peaceful, more lucrative time. The roaring twenties heralded the start of a period of contrasts; anyone with money increased their prosperity, but the poor continued to realise a life of scarcity and restriction. The rich got richer, as they say.

Sponsorship was rare in the 1920s, but the 30s saw an increase in golf sponsorship in general with Southport emerging as one of the leading venues for professional golfing tournaments. Southport's first publicity manager, Thomas Edwin Wolstenholme, who had been influential in establishing the Southport Flower Show in 1924, persuaded the local authority to set up a Golf Tournament Committee on which sat two representatives from each of the four major local golf clubs. The committee were responsible for launching Southport as an influential area for golfing per se. Effectively, this was the birth of Southport as the capital of what would become England's Golfing Coast.

The period before World War 1 saw a lot of development in Southport, and various entertainments were created in the area. However, Teddy and his friends enjoyed the simpler pleasures in life, such as walking along Southport promenade or strolling down Lord Street. Being inherently shy, he wasn't particularly interested in girls and took a back seat, unlike his friends Tom and David who delighted in flirting and making the girls blush.

A favourite pastime for them was boating on the Botanical Gardens lake, one of the main features in the park in the Churchtown area of the town. It was on one such outing, on a cold spring Sunday in 1920, that Ted fell in love for the first - and only - time.

The trees were just beginning to bud and birds were involved in mating rituals and singing aloud. The boating lake was shallow but had a thin skin of algae and debris coating the water. Ted and his friends waited patiently while the queue dwindled down, others joining it at the back.

As he was getting into the boat it started to drift away from the side. With one foot in the boat and one on the side, he lost his balance and fell with a huge splash, face first into the water. It was impossible not to notice him and a cheer went up from the people who were waiting their turn for a boat. Ted swore and sat in the water with algae, weeds and water dripping off his hair and clothing. His friends and most of the queue laughed loudly at him.

The young woman at the front, however, looked concerned, and their eyes locked as she moved forward to offer her hand to steady him while he scrambled up on to the bank.

"I'm Margaret," she said shyly. "Can I help you up? This is my friend Bridgette." But Bridgette was falling about laughing and couldn't contain herself. Tom and David too had tears of laughter rolling down their cheeks as, with water pouring from his clothing, he scrambled out of the dirty pool and stood in front of her.

Margaret's hair was the colour of his mother's and was pinned up under her straw bonnet. Her eyes were the deepest brown and she blushed as he smiled and held her gaze. Although immaculately clean, her coat was slightly worn at the cuffs and there was a small patch at the hem of her dress. She was softly spoken with a slight cockney lilt that he found enchanting. He asked if she came to the gardens regularly, but she shook her head and explained that she didn't go out that often as she was in service locally. She had been orphaned in the war and brought from London to Manchester and only recently moved to Southport. She had made friends with Bridgette in Manchester and it was only by chance Bridgette had called on her today - her first rest day since starting work in the house - and had asked if she would come to the park with her. Bridgette was going back to Manchester later in the day and, because Margaret was under the ward of her employees, probably wouldn't be allowed to come over on her own.

After introducing himself, Ted wanted to stay and talk, but he needed to go home and change and it was too late for him to come back that afternoon. He asked if there was any chance she would be there on the following Sunday.

"I really can't say," she answered. "It depends if I can get time off work and if I can come on over." Reluctantly he pulled himself away to head off for the long walk back home. Their eyes locked and as they turned away from each other he gestured to his friends that his heart was coming out of his body. Bridgette saw him and giggled.

"Teddy Fyles," Margaret said sternly, "I've got eyes in the back of my head and I saw that."

Ted felt a shiver go up and down his spine and as he leaned towards his mates he said, "Don't look now, but that's the girl I'm going to marry."

The next week it rained. But Ted, now suffering with a cold from walking the three miles back home in soaking clothes, still persuaded his friends to go back to the Gardens. They sat in the café from where they could see the entrance and the boating lake. Each time someone looking remotely like Margaret walked in the gate his heart jumped, only to be bitterly disappointed. Hours later, realising it was too late for her to appear that day, they left, but he was determined to visit every weekend that he could. Due to his commitments at the club, he couldn't make it every week, but each free Sunday his friends indulged him and they returned so that he could look for her again.

There was no sign of her until one Sunday, some months later, Margaret, a young man and older woman walked past Ted and sat on the seat by the aviary just opposite the café.

His heart thumped as he strived to get her attention, but she wouldn't look at him. The older woman seemed to be in charge and looked fearsome in her Sunday regalia. She was obviously better off than Margaret. The bottom of her dress was edged with lace and she had on a velvet coat and an expensive-looking hat adorned with feathers and silk flowers.

In those days, it wasn't acceptable to get friendly with some young man the family hadn't been introduced to and Ted racked his brains for a way to meet her again. He thought he would go mad if he didn't speak to her soon and he longed to look once more into her beautiful hazel eyes.

The chance to meet her again came about through a most unexpected opportunity when, a few months later, a new junior green keeper was appointed at Birkdale. The head keeper introduced Ted as one of their most valued employees and asked him to show James around the club and grounds. They hit it off immediately and soon built an excellent working relationship. Although he would not be privy to the information immediately, it transpired that James was the son of the couple who Margaret worked for. James' father Peter was a member of the club and had welcomed the opportunity for James to become one of the keepers, to get some life experience and potentially work towards head keeper when the current one retired.

Ted and James became good friends and a few months later James invited Ted to a family gathering to celebrate Peter's 60th birthday. Margaret had also been invited, not as an employee but to attend socially.

Ted knocked politely and when the door was opened he walked through the gloomy hallway which was lit by a single gas light. He could hear soft laughter in a room at the far end of the passageway and he felt irrationally nervous as he entered the parlour. He had caddied for Peter on many occasions and cleaned his clubs afterwards. Peter regarded Ted with affection, as did many club members, but it was somewhat intimidating to be asked to a social event in the prestigious Hillside area of the town.

Margaret sat with her back to him and as she turned for James to introduce them, Ted froze as their eyes met and he realised who she was. Margaret almost dropped her cup and it took some control to get back her composure. He mumbled a brief hello and felt his knees wobble as she continued to hold his gaze. He was glad when they were called to the table for the meal as he wasn't sure his legs would keep him up much longer.

They sat on opposite sides of the dining table and kept catching each other's eye, trying not to make their mutual attraction obvious. After the meal, they left the table to take part in the entertainment - there was an upright piano which James's father played expertly and everyone joined in singing along. Ted ensured he was standing close to Margaret, and when they accidentally brushed against each other they both felt that charge of electricity that lovers have experienced since time immemorial.

Ted became a regular visitor to the house and after some time asked James's father if he could take Margaret out. Being a favourite of his and having long since recognised Ted's good character and honesty, he said he would be delighted providing he looked after her and didn't keep her out too late. He pointed out that she had work to do and he wouldn't tolerate Ted interfering with this on any basis.

From the moment that Ted and Margaret started seeing each other they spent as much time together as possible, and before long he had asked her to marry him. Naturally, he discussed it with Peter, which was protocol as she was still in his service, but he readily agreed. Thus it was that the spring of 1922 not only realised the development of the links at Birkdale, but also saw Ted and Margaret attending a quiet ceremony in their local church. She wore her mother's wedding dress and they had just one bridesmaid, Bridgette, who wore her own best dress. The reception was held at James' house and they had a small wedding cake which was baked and exquisitely decorated by Ted's aunt.

His father gave Ted his grandmother's wedding ring, which some years previously had been handed down to him. It was just a little too big for Margaret's finger, but she loved it and wouldn't have wanted another one even if they could have afforded it. Both families had many relatives, but they kept the guests down to a bare minimum to save on the catering, which Margaret's paternal aunt provided as a wedding present. Although Peter had insisted on contributing towards the wedding, it was a fairly meagre affair, but nonetheless lively.

After the wedding breakfast, everyone gathered around the upright and they sang the romantic songs of the day. The couple spent the night together in Ted's aunt's house - she kindly stayed with her sister - and after the wedding they moved in with his parents, as did many young couples in post-Victorian England. It wasn't ideal, especially as they had Billy, James and Margaret, the first three of their eight children while still living with his parents. Consequently, they applied for a council house, which they were allocated in 1926. The couple loved having their own home and would remain there until their deaths many years later.

25 Suffolk Road was located on a newly built council estate not far from his parent's home and just over a mile from the golf club. Their moving in coincided with the birth of Alfie, their fourth child, and they quickly settled into a routine of domesticity. Inevitably, with eight children being born in short succession, there was never enough money to go around and all the children were expected to contribute from an early age.

Ted took all his boys to the club at one point or another to introduce them to the sport, and Alfie in particular took an interest in what his father did at work. He would listen intently to tales Ted told him about the comings and goings of the players at Birkdale, and of the various tournaments Ted would hear of and discuss with the players and his colleagues, or read about in the golfing magazines and papers at the club. He quickly got caught up in the excitement of the development of the club and the hustle and bustle when there was an important game on.

In 1930, Southport Corporation and the *Daily Dispatch* sponsored a £1,500 professional golf tournament in the area, the two-day qualifiers taking place at the Hillside, Hesketh, and S&A golf clubs, the ensuing finals to be held at Birkdale. It is reported that Southport Corporation were praised for the tournament but that the *Daily Dispatch* was left with a loss of £1,000 and subsequently withdrew its support.

The following year, the Corporation was joined in sponsorship by the Dunlop Rubber company when the Dunlop-Southport tournament was initiated with the introduction of the 1,500 guineas Professional Tournament. In subsequent years, the qualifiers for the annual event would be shared between the four major clubs. Henry Cotton would be a major figure, winning in 1931, 1932 and going on to win the Open Championship in 1934, 1937 and 1948.

The 1933 Ryder Cup was held in Southport, but it caused quite a dilemma as to which course should hold it as both the Hesketh and Birkdale courses were in development following their purchase by Southport Corporation. The prestigious S&A was finally chosen as the preferred course. This turned out to be a wise choice as the Prince of Wales attended the tournament, in his capacity as President of the Professional Golfers Association, to present the Cup to Britain. The 1933 competition was such a success that, once more, the club was chosen to host the 1937 tournament. Birkdale continued to develop and the now famous two-storey Art Deco clubhouse with its elegant lounges, was subsequently opened on July 6th, 1935. It was located behind the new 18th hole and is an impressive sight to this day.

When Ted was caddying, he would be up early to join the queue of willing locals waiting to be paired up with their 'man.' He called it bagging, and Alf couldn't wait until he could go to the club and take his turn to 'bag.'

When he was old enough, Ted took Alfie to one side saying, "Right, lad, tomorrow there's a big competition on and there's a couple of Americans coming over, not to mention the other professional players who will need a good caddy. I'm working, but you make your way to the club and tell the pro I sent you. You can earn a few bob for your mother, but remember, no moaning or complaining, no swearing or cursing - I've built myself a good reputation and I don't want you spoiling it for me. Be respectful, do what your man tells you and you will be alright. If he wins, you might even earn some spending money for yourself."

Alfie did as his father said and eight o'clock the next morning saw him running and stumbling his way through the streets and over the fields until he came to the Southport to Liverpool railway track. Carefully he manoeuvred his way over the live rail then finally slipped into the grounds of the club.

It was a beautiful spring day, which promised to turn into the best day of the year so far. Birds sang and the smell of the newly cut greens and the sight of emerging spring shoots made Alf glad to be alive. He was out of breath from running so far, and when he arrived there was a crowd of men and youths already waiting to be picked for caddying. Slightly built Alfie only just reached the chest of some of the men, but he stood his ground and waited in the line with the others.

When the pro arrived, Alfie dashed over, blurting out who he was and that his father had sent him especially. The man towered over him, but was impressed by his tenacity and obvious enthusiasm. He was on good terms with Ted and smiled as he bent to look Alfie in the face.

"Well, if your dad says you can caddy, I don't think it's my place to say no, is it, son? Have you caddied before?"

Alfie hadn't caddied before and didn't know what to expect, but what harm could he come to carrying a few clubs around a golf course on such a beautiful day? Slowly he shook his head, afraid that the Pro might change his mind, but no, he paired Alfie up with Reg Brown, a lesser-known player who he knew wouldn't be so hard on the boy. Alfie bounded over to the player and greeted him respectfully as his father had instructed.

"Good morning, Mr Brown sir, I'm Alfie Fyles and I'm going to be your caddy for the day. What would you like me to do?"

Amused, the player pointed to his golf bag leaning up against the club house. "Well, young Alfie Fyles, I need you to carry that bag around with me so I can use the right club for the shot I'm about to make. If you do that I will pay you one and threepence, and if you clean my clubs and shoes afterwards I will give you another sixpence - how does that sound?"

How did it sound? Alfie had only ever earned pennies doing jobs for the neighbours and to earn one and ninepence for a day was unbelievable. He walked over and considered the bag, which was nearly as tall as he was. He went to pick it up but hadn't expected it to weigh so much. He wrestled with it and eventually hoisted it up onto his shoulder, almost falling over in the process.

For the first few holes Alf struggled, and by the 14th hole his shoulder was quite tender so he kept hoisting the bag from shoulder to shoulder to even out the load, all the way to the 18th.

Perhaps it was the smell of the turf, the atmosphere, the solitude, the blue skies. Perhaps it was the intrigue as his man took a club, carefully considered it and looked down the shaft, then took the weight in his hand - Alfie didn't know what it was, but he had been brought up on tales of famous names including Henry Cotton, Alf Perry and Alf Padgham, who had all played in major tournaments, and he began to daydream. The match was suddenly transformed into the Open with Reg being a putt away from winning. As they walked all the way down the fairway, the crowds standing on the sides of the sandhills clapped and cheered them on. When Reg sank the winning putt, he turned to Alf, shaking his hand and thanking him for his excellent knowledge and support.

It would be a memory that stayed with Alfie all his life, and coming back to stern reality he realised that he hadn't felt his shoulder hurting since the 17th.

Something triggered inside him that day that made him realise a caddying career was exactly what he wanted out of life. When he got home he proudly held out his hand to give his mother the money. She took it and gave him sixpence back. He winced as his father put his hand on his shoulder to tell him he had done a good job, and his mother made him take off his shirt, gasping as she saw his chafed and bruised skin.

As she bathed it Ted said, "Get used to it, lad, it's the best work you can get in this area."

"That's Ok, dad, I won the Open today and I didn't moan or complain once, even when the bag slipped off and it hurt like hell.

I'm going to be a professional caddy one day and win the Open for real."

"I know, son, I know." And he turned away so his son couldn't see the tears rolling down his cheek.

3

Teamwork to World War 2

In 1931, the International Olympic Committee awarded the 1936 Summer Olympics to Berlin: officially known as the Games of the XI Olympiad, the decision signaled Germany's return to the world community after its isolation in the aftermath of defeat in World War 1. Two years later, Adolf Hitler became chancellor of Germany and saw the ensuing Olympics as an opportunity to demonstrate German superiority and to prove the reality of the master race. On August 1st, 1936, Hitler presided over the opening ceremony, and the Games commenced.

In an Olympics where Jesse Owens won four gold medals in the sprint and long jump, despite Nazi attempts to stop his participating, Karl Henkell, the so-called 'Golf Fuhrer', dreamed up the idea of a golf tournament to be played not as a part of, but in conjunction with the Games.

On August 26th, ten days after the Olympics ended, the tournament commenced with Tom Thirsk and Arnold Bentley representing the England golf squad. Arnold and his brother Harry of Southport's Hesketh Golf Club were two of the most celebrated pre-war amateur golfers, collecting a variety of trophies in their wake, and although they played well, the host team, after ending the first three rounds with a three-stroke lead, were the favourites to win. However, Bentley and teammate Tom turned the tables to take a four-shot winning lead.

It appears that this upset Adolf, because he was on his way to present the appropriately named Hitler Trophy to the German team as everyone was convinced that they were in line for victory. Upon receiving the news from Foreign Minister von Ribbentrop, a furious Hitler did a U-turn and returned from whence he came.

The Hitler Trophy, which is an impressive brass salver inlaid with eight large amber discs, was awarded to the British team, but it went missing for a long time, being returned to the Hesketh - its spiritual home - in recent years.

The England team also received a small fir tree as part of their prize and it was planted on a sandhill behind the flagstaff at the club. When hostilities broke out, members of the Hesketh used the tree as a urinal, but despite this, it continues to thrive!

The council houses in Suffolk Road were soon filled with families, and the other boys who lived in the street latched on to the fact that there were easy pickings to be made at the golf course and many of them raised much-needed money to eke out the family finances. Albert, Kenny, and David, Alfie's younger brothers, were also expected to contribute and the other lads in the street would knock and ask, 'Hey, Alfie, anything going on at the club tomorrow? I'll come with you'.

Before too long there was a regular team of boys standing in line waiting to be chosen; their young lives were stippled with competitions and tournaments and they picked up lots of invaluable tips which made them the best caddies in their field. However, four of them, neighbours in the same small road in Birkdale, would go on to caddy for some of the most famous golfers and celebrities in the world.

The four were Alfie Fyles, Albert Fyles, Bobby Leigh and Teddy Halsall; they would travel globally to 'win' some of the most prestigious matches of the 20th century, including 10 British Opens, numerous Walker Cups, Penfold Tournaments, Alcans, PGA Match Plays and Piccadilly Match Plays, amongst other competitions. Alfie's younger brother David was also a formidable caddy in his own right, but didn't achieve the heady heights that the others managed in their careers.

It didn't matter what the competition was, whether amateur, professional, ladies, gents or pro-am, the Birkdale Boys as they came to be known, if they were free would line up at all the local clubs - Birkdale, Hillside, S&A, the Municipal, the Hesketh, and would travel as far afield as their funds would allow.

Teddy Halsall always insisted that, for him, his mother was the driving force behind his success.

"Come on, you lazy lot!" Mrs Halsall shouted up the stairs. It was seven o'clock in the morning and if she was up, everyone in the house was up. "Get out of that bed, NOW."

"Oh, come on, Mam, just five more minutes."

"Never mind five more minutes, that won't buy the baby a new pair of shoes."

Silence ensued.

"But, Mam, we don't have a baby."

"**UP. NOW.** Don't mess me about or you will feel my shoe on your backside. Boys, get yourselves on that golf course. You know there's a competition on today. Get some money earned. I can't afford to feed the ten of you. Girls, there's washing to be done and I need the grate cleaning. Then there's dinner to be made. Move it."

Come sunshine or rain, they were all expected to pull their weight. As the youngest of ten, Teddy Halsall was somewhat spoiled by the older children, but had to contribute all the same. His caddying career started around 1948 when he and Albert Fyles were both eleven, although it had to be in their spare time as the 1921 Education Act had raised the school-leaving age to fourteen. They were in the same class at school, so developed a close friendship which endured through school and into adulthood. When Teddy started caddying, he could earn three shillings and sixpence a round. In a good week, he could earn six pounds, which was more than his older brother was earning doing a full-time job.

Alfie in his youth got a job at the dairy farm in Birkdale village. His duties were to deliver the milk in the daytime then look after the horse at the end of the day. He had to ensure it was fed and stabled for the night, although occasionally he would take it back home with him to his mum and dad's house in Suffolk Road.

On one such occasion, he left it tethered in the back garden so it could graze on the back lawn. The horse seemed happy enough and Alf, checking the horse was Ok before he went to bed, when he looked through the kitchen window could see its silhouette in the moonlight as it continued to graze on the lush summer grass. At 7.00 the next morning, though, he was awakened by his mother screaming at him to come down and sort the damned thing out. Not only had the horse eaten its way through the grass but it had eaten virtually every flower in Ted's well-maintained and precious garden, including his prize dahlias. Alfie, half dressed and shoeless, scurried out to take hold of the tether and guide it away from the bush.

"And don't you dare bring that ruddy thing home here again," were the last words he heard from Margaret that day. "Your dad says the glue factory is waiting for it right now."

It was ironical that, when renting a flat in the 1980s, it overlooked the same dairy farm he had worked on before World War 2.

Jackie Leigh, usually known as Bobby, was born in 1939, just before the start of World War 2. He joined the Southport caddying circuit in 1949 when he was ten, the same year that Tom Watson was born.

Life was hard, and life in a working-class family meant children had to face harsh realities and grow up early in many ways. In other ways, it was a slower, more innocent and peaceful age, although there is no doubt that the peace was shattered by the arrival of World War 2 in September 1939. Birkdale Golf Club was nominated as the venue for the 1940 Open Championship but the outbreak of the war meant the Championship was cancelled.

As part of the war effort, many of the local clubs allowed the grazing of animals on the course and/or turned over parts of the course to the growing of vegetables. Hillside allowed the grazing of sheep on some parts of its course, although a fence was duly erected around the greens to protect them. Grazing the sheep effectively saved on manpower by reducing the mowing needs of the course during this period and, presumably, the ensuing fertilizer would nourish and promote healthy growth. However, it is worthy of note that a new rule was introduced:

Any ball lying in a hole or scrape made by a sheep in a bunker can be lifted out and placed without penalty.

The club also grew vegetables on their allotment, which was situated close to the old 3rd green, and they continued to grow produce until the 1950s when the allotment was turned into a nursery.

The coastline off Southport and Formby, running into the Liverpool estuary with its shifting sands and unpredictable sandbanks has seen many shipwrecks, and on October 17th, 1939, the *Ionic Star* ran aground. In November of the same year, the cargo/passenger *SS Pegu* was beached on a sandbank late at night in the Crosby Channel, carrying around 103 people. The ship was trying to get into Liverpool to pick up cotton and goods to take to Rangoon. Being the start of the war, the navigation buoys in the channel were switched off, so she was unable to navigate safely into the dock. She carried a variety of goods including a consignment of whiskey that was washed up on the shore and which proved too much of a temptation for local father and son, Henry and Ralph Dewsbury; they were accused of stealing two bottles to the value of £1. 9s. 6d. When the police visited the couple's home, 'The two were unconscious on the floor and an empty, sand-coated bottle of whiskey was found at their side'.

In truth, the wrecks along the coast and the rubble from the bombed buildings in Liverpool that was dumped along the shoreline around Waterloo, drew hundreds of sightseers, and many local youths could be seen walking along the shore, or travelling from Southport to Waterloo on the Cheshire Lines train to ogle the sites and explore the coastline for artefacts and other useful items that had been washed ashore.

Located on the outskirts of Liverpool and having a major munitions factory, Southport got badly bombed, and the Blitz of Christmas 1940 saw many buildings wrecked and hundreds of casualties and fatalities. The bombs were no respecter of age, socio-economic status, creed, colour or disability, and even the Home for Blind Babies in Birkdale came under fire.

When fifteen-year-old Alfie left school in May 1941 he considered it his duty to sign up and go to war. Brother Billy had joined the Navy at the outbreak and Alf had a notion he could enlist and meet up with him. He talked to his mates about joining up and spoke to his father one day when his mother was out of the house.

"Dad, I've decided to join the Navy."

"I don't think you're old enough, Alf."

"I'll get around that, Dad - Fred from our school signed up for the Army a couple of months ago and he got in. Apparently, people lie about their age all the time. There's got to be a way. There's a recruitment office in Liverpool - I'll go first thing Monday. It will be great to meet up with our Billy again. I can't wait."

Forty-three-year-old Ted smiled at his son but inwardly it hurt that he himself was now too old to sign up. What the hell? Let him live the dream if he wants to, he thought. He was proud of his son for wanting to sign up, but felt glad that particular dream would probably not come true.

"Just don't tell your mother now, she'll only worry."

Monday morning saw Alf waiting for the recruitment office to open. Respectful as ever, he chatted at length to the officer in charge, asking questions about the Navy and getting increasingly more enthusiastic. In fact, he asked if he could sign up there and then.

"Sorry, Alf, we aren't taking volunteers right now. Under the National Services Act, the government are only conscripting men into the forces. They will contact you when the time is right."

Alfie was devastated. He walked up to the docks where a warship was anchored. Sailors milled around, cleaning, stocking up and generally preparing for the ship's launch. Oh, how he longed to be aboard. He stood watching for hours until he realised he was shivering with cold, disappointment and hunger. He got the train back to Southport and bought himself a meal in the station canteen before taking a slow walk back home. When he arrived, he was still shivering. His mother had already gone to bed, but his father was sitting at the kitchen table, reading the newspaper.

"Well, son, how did you go on?"

"They aren't taking anybody right now, Dad." The pair looked at each other for a few moments, Alfie with misted eyes.

"Do you want a cup of tea, lad?"

Alfie nodded his head, too emotional to speak.

"One for you, one for me and one for the pot."

The sweet strong tea served to thaw him out and they drank in silence. Ted took the cups and washed them up before heading towards the stairs.

"Probably for the best, Alf. It would break your mother's heart if anything happened to you."

Determined to do his bit, however, he applied instead to join the Merchant Navy and signed up in 1942 as soon as he was sixteen. It wasn't the forces but it was the next best thing.

While no major tournaments were played throughout the war, many local clubs stayed open and Richmond Golf Club in Surrey mocked the Nazi regime by issuing the following tongue in cheek rules, advising players what to do if bombed during a game:

1. Players are asked to collect Bomb and Shrapnel splinters to save these causing damage to the mowing machines.
2. In competitions, during gunfire, or while bombs are falling, players may take cover without penalty for ceasing play.
3. The positions of known delayed-action bombs are marked by red flags placed at reasonably, but not guaranteed safe distance therefrom.
4. Shrapnel/and/or bomb splinters on the Fairways, or in Bunkers within a club's length of a ball may be moved without penalty, and no penalty shall be incurred if a ball is thereby caused to move accidentally.
5. A ball moved by enemy action may be replaced, or if lost or destroyed, a ball may be dropped not nearer the hole without penalty.
6. A ball lying in a crater may be lifted and dropped not nearer the hole, preserving the line to the hole without penalty.
7. A player whose stroke is affected by the simultaneous explosion of a bomb may play another ball from the same place. Penalty, one stroke.

Some golf was played locally, and when Alf came home on leave he continued to caddy and always considered that he would become a professional at some point. It was about this time that he started considering yardages, i.e. working out how far it was between one point and another on the course, as he realised that winning was less about good luck and more about strategy and mathematical calculation. Teddy Halsall, Albert and Bobby Leigh were still at school throughout the war years and life went on; they were just normal kids, pretending to be soldiers and following the progression of the war, wishing they could follow Alfie's lead. Many men from their neighbourhood didn't return home from the war and the boys lost uncles, brothers and close friends. Ironically Fred, who had lied about his age and enlisted at fifteen, was killed in action six months later, and Billy was lost at sea before the end of the war without ever meeting up with Alf.

A detachment of American soldiers was based at RAF Burtonwood in Warrington, not far from Southport, and many a local female family member or close friend was lost to them as well. The GIs brought over a ready supply of chewing gum, stockings, chocolate etc. to turn a young lady's head, and they could always afford to take a girl to the pictures or out for the day.

4

Changes

September 1945 saw the end of the war, but Alf stayed in the Merchant Navy until 1947. One night he was in the Mason's Arms with a couple of mates who worked on Peter Pan's Playground, a smaller version of the famous Southport fairground, located just over the Marine Lake Bridge.

"Well, lads, I suppose I'd better look for a job now I'm out. How goes it at the fairground?"

"Great, mate. Money's rubbish, but you can make a few quid when no one's looking, and the girls flock round you like flies around shit."

Alfie thought it would be better than nothing. There wasn't a lot of work around since the end of the war although he worked on the building sites in the winter and continued to caddy at the weekends when possible.

He got the job at Peter Pan's and mid-season he heard that the manager at Southport Pleasureland was looking for someone to work on the motordrome ride. He hadn't particularly heard of a motordrome, but he could drive a van, so he said, 'Think I'll go and have a look, lads. How hard can it be?' Peter Pan's didn't open until 10.00 so Alf and two friends walked over to the manager's office at the fairground.

"I heard you were looking for a driver for your motordrome, mate."

"And you think that could be you, do you, son?"

"I don't see why not. I've got a licence and I've been driving all sorts while I was in the Navy, and I've ridden the speedway."

"Do you know what they call the motordrome, son?"

"Er ... a motordrome?"

His mates sniggered by the door.

Bristling, the manager spoke slowly and deliberately. "They call the motordrome the 'Wall of Death'. Come with me and have a look and if you think you're still up to it, I'll give you a try."

They walked over to a huge wooden structure and all four of them climbed the steps to the platform at the top. The manager pointed down over the top and inside. It had completely vertical thirty foot walls which curved slightly inwards at the bottom leading onto a wooden floor. It looked like huge wooden mixing bowl, but was approximately forty feet in diameter. Driving at speed until the rider reached the top was a death-defying feat as the rider would be vertical and only held up by centrifugal force.

"I've got a regular guy who drives for me, but my second driver mis-gauged the speed a couple of weeks ago and fell from the top - broke God knows how many bones and made a hell of a mess of the bike. I was hoping he would come with me when I opened here but he won't be getting on a motor bike for some time, believe me. Tell you what, why don't you get yourself on that bike over there and give it a go if you're still interested."

Alf was filled with exhilaration and terror. Like all the others he had worked on the speedway, but it wasn't the same as riding a bike horizontally on a wooden wall. However, he couldn't lose face in front of his mates, so feigning confidence he said, "OK, mate. Where's the key?"

He started the engine and revved up loudly. The manager opened the door into the arena and waved Alfie inside. Slowly he drove around the base, building up speed and mounting the curve. Soon he was up to speed and about two feet off the floor. He continued to gain height until he was about half way up the wall. The feeling was amazing. Gut-churning excitement now overtook any fear he had and he didn't want to stop, but the manager was gesturing madly for him to come off the wall. The coming down was much worse than going up. Until now he had just revved up and gone for it. Now he had to gauge the right speed to get him back down without stalling or falling. He pulled in the throttle and made it safely back onto the floor with the smell of petrol in his nose and the sound of the engine, magnified tenfold due to the proximity of the walls, buzzing in his ears.

"Well?"

He got the job as second man for the regular driver, doing the maintenance on the bikes and motordrome when he wasn't driving. Even so, Alf still retained his lifelong ambition to be a caddy; any other work he did was just filling in time until he could caddy again.

Working the fast rides at the fairground always drew a crowd of girls, who flirted and chatted, hanging around sometimes all day long. The ride operators could go out with any one of a hundred girls and they frequently took advantage of the situation. Alfie, like any hot-blooded young man, didn't necessarily pass up the chance of such willing companionship. But first and last, he was a gentleman, and anyone who knew him considered his charm to be one of his most endearing characteristics.

One day, a group of young women on a day's outing at the fair, were waiting to watch the next Wall of Death show. Alf recognised one of them because she worked at Peter Pan's and stood out from the other hangers-on that the boys found themselves knee-deep in all day long. She was confident and didn't take any nonsense.

Alf asked the regular driver if he could go on next.

"If you want to, mate, but just remember it's been raining so the wheels are going to be lethal today. Take it easy till the tyres have dried out. OK?"

"Yeah. No problem."

Alf couldn't wait to show off. He revved up outside the dome then drove inside, stopping for dramatic effect as the crowd whooped and clapped. He pushed the bike around a couple of laps but the tyres were still not quite dry. As he revved up and started to mount the incline, the bike went one way and he went the other. A huge groan went up, then silence as he lay winded in the middle of the floor. As he got his breath back he stretched and hauled himself up on his knees. When he stood up and moved towards the bike the crowd realised the drama was over and started climbing back down the stairs, most of them demanding their money back.

"Don't go, the show will be back on in ten minutes!" shouted the owner. "We'll just get the main driver in the dome and we'll be up and running again."

Some people stayed, and as Alfie hauled the bike back out of the arena the boss demanded to know what had happened, roasting him for not taking more caution. Alf was only half listening, though, as he saw the group of girls he had noticed earlier making their way to the carousel a few yards away.

"Sorry, Bert - it won't happen again."

"You bet it won't. You're on maintenance only till you can learn to master the finer points of The Wall."

Alf told the manager he needed to go for a break and walked over to the carousel the girls were heading for. He was aching all over and thought he had probably broken a rib, but he wanted to speak to the girl he had seen in the crowd.

"These ladies are with me, George." And so they got a free ride.

Pat looked up and said 'thanks'. She turned towards her friends and they laughed at his forthrightness.

When the ride stopped, he offered her his hand as she stepped down. But he didn't let go, and slowly drew her hand up to his lips and kissed it.

"I'm Alfie, do you come here often?"

It was corny and she retorted, "That's got nothing to do with you. I go where I want when I want, cheeky." Realising who he was, she added, "Are you OK? You went with a hell of a bang in there."

"Think I might have broken something - how about checking for me?"

"Get lost," she smiled, pushing him, making him wince. "Oh God, I'm so sorry."

"Well, you could at least let me buy you a drink for causing me such pain - and what is such a vision of loveliness doing tonight?"

"I'm washing my hair."

"And tomorrow night?"

"Washing it again in case I didn't do it properly the first time."

When Pat laughed, her face lit up and her eyes twinkled, making him even more determined not to let her leave without getting to know her. She was funny, whereas most of the other girls pouted and looked surly.

She agreed to have a coffee and he followed them to the café, sitting in between her and her friends so she had to look round him if she wanted to speak to them. 'Moonlight and Roses' came on the radio and by the time they parted he had arranged to meet up with her again the following Tuesday evening. They eventually adopted the tune as their song, and whenever they heard it would share a special moment, even years after they had split up.

Alfie took Pat to see *The Ghost and Mrs Muir* featuring Gene Tierney and Rex Harrison and they held hands all through the film. Afterwards they went for a drink and then caught the bus back to her house. Being the gentleman that he was, Alfie took Pat's hand and kissed it. He asked if he could see her again, and from that moment they shared as much time as possible, going to the cinema, walking down the pier hand in hand, sitting on the promenade watching the sun go down, and dancing at the local dance halls. Alf walked home after their first date, savouring the cool night air and warm glow inside him, feeling pleased with himself that the evening had gone so well.

They couldn't get enough of each other, and they fell into a safe, sweet partnership which was based on respect and love. For the first few months of seeing each other they kept to kissing. Both wanted to go further, of course, but they refrained because in those days it wasn't socially correct to jump into bed together.

One cold, crisp Saturday outside of the golfing season they stood by the bandstand outside the Town Hall on Lord Street. As they watched and listened to Betty Driver (later of Coronation Street fame) singing with the Henry Hall Band, Alfie suddenly excused himself and ran over to the florist shop on the opposite corner. He came back a few minutes later, hands behind his back and nodded to the band master.

The tempo changed and the band started playing 'Moonlight and Roses'. Alfie took Pat's hand as he knelt in front of her.

"Alfie?" Pat was bemused and a little embarrassed.

"What are you doing in June next year?" He held out the rose as he kissed the back of her hand.

"Washing my hair, of course."

"Well, when it's dry, how about becoming Mrs Alfie Fyles?"

Pat filled up. She still wasn't sure if he was joking or not and found it hard to speak.

"Are you kidding me, Alfie?"

"No, Pat, I'm not. Will you do me the honour of marrying me?"

"I would love to, Mr Fyles," she crooned, and they walked back to her house ensconced in each other, talking chitchat until they got to her front door. They kissed passionately before Alf left to walk back to his own house.

Floating on air and impervious to the northerly wind which had turned the night bitterly cold, he let himself in. His mother was sleeping upstairs and he carefully removed his cap and scarf before turning to his father, with whom he had an outstanding relationship. Whenever he had a problem or an issue or just something good to share, Ted was the first person he wanted to talk to.

"I've asked Pat to marry me."

Ted was taken aback. "But you've only been seeing her a few months, son."

"I know, but she makes me laugh, Dad, and I can't imagine not being with her."

"But how will you cope moneywise, Alf? Will you have enough to live on, on your wage?"

In all honesty, Alf didn't know the answer to those questions but he was determined to make the marriage work. They planned the wedding on a shoestring, as had his mother and father so many years before, and Alfie was prepared to do whatever he needed to keep Pat. As they started planning for the wedding they realised they might have to cut corners in some areas, but it didn't matter because they were hopelessly in love. The summer and autumn raced past and Alfie worked all the hours he could to make money for the wedding. He continued to live at home, spent as much time with Pat as he could, had the odd bet on the horses and went out with his mates.

It wasn't unusual for the lads to go out and have a few pints, then go back to one of their houses and sleep there for the night. On Christmas Eve in the winter of 1947, Skid, one of a group of friends living with the family of his half-brother in Broome Road (or Brush Alley as it was affectionately known), together with Alfie and Skid's brother Joey, went to the George public house on the corner of Duke Street and Cemetery Road, then headed off back home to Joey's house. All were, shall we say, a little merry!

The pubs closed at 10.00 pm in those days and there were no food outlets available to get anything to eat. Slipping and sliding and with much bravado, the trio made their way back home, singing Christmas carols along the way. All the boys were hungry and they crept into the house intending to ask Joey's mother if they could make a sandwich. However, everyone had gone to bed and although his mum had plenty of food in for the festivities, what assailed their nostrils was the smell of the main course, freshly cooked chicken, which was still hot to the touch. Turkeys hadn't been introduced into Britain at that point but Mrs Ball had done the family proud with a beautiful plump chicken and they wouldn't go hungry - that at least was the theory.

In all fairness, in their inebriated state none of them could remember who suggested it first, but one of them sidled over to the cooling chicken and pulled off a small piece of skin.

"Oh, Lord, that's good." He picked off another piece and one of the wings. "Mum won't miss one tiny little wing."

Within minutes, the three of them were pulling off bits of the chicken, devouring the lot with relish.

It didn't take long and they looked down at the decimated carcase with satisfaction until they realised what they had done. Panic set in and they fervently discussed what they could do with the evidence that would provide a feasible explanation. Mrs Ball would kill them if she found out it was them.

They crept upstairs, hushing and shushing and encouraging each other not to wake the rest of the household, and then, carefully but deliberately, hid the bones under the pillow of Joey's younger, teenage brother, Ray, who slept innocently through the whole ordeal.

The brothers piled into Skid's room and Alfie fell asleep on the settee in the front room.

Next morning, Joey senior was met at the bottom of the stairs by a tearful Mrs Ball who lamented the fact that she no longer had any decent meat for the family's Christmas lunch and that she would have to open a couple of tins of Spam.

Joey senior ranted and raved, as you would expect, and demanded that the perpetrator own up to their crime.

It was a tense few hours until Joey decided to search the house to look for any evidence which might indicate who it was who had eaten the chicken. He barked to each one to look in this or that and eventually the evidence did indeed present itself.

It is irrelevant who found the bones. But found they were under young Ray's pillow where the lads had hidden them. He suffered the consequences by means of his father's strap and was devastated as he protested his innocence, which was not proven until about twenty years later when Skid, Alfie and Joey confessed to Ray one night - probably on another frosty Christmas Eve.

In the spring of 1948, Skid and Alfie, being broke at the time, realised there was easy money to be made if they were a bit crafty. Joey Ball senior had buried a piece of piping a yard deep into the ground in the back garden so that the top of it was virtually level with the grass and, when he had any extra money would drop the odd half-crown into it as a rainy-day fund. Skid and Alf couldn't easily dig the pipe up but they had worked out that if they tied a piece of string to one of the children's toy arrows which came with a sucker attached at one end, then wet the sucker, they could shoot the arrow down into the void and, with patience, they could carefully pull out some of the coins from the bottom of the pipe.

When Mr. Ball eventually dug up the pipe, expecting there to be quite a few pounds inside it, he was disappointed to see just a few silver coins shining up at him. He did work out who had purloined the money, but Alfie, being a charmer, soon won him over and, between Skid and Alfie's caddying, he was paid back triple-fold over the following years.

The Amateur Championship was the first post-war championship to be played at Birkdale. It took place in May 1946 with James Bruen and Robert Sweeney contesting the final. With Bruen realising a margin of 4 and 3 (being 4 holes up with 3 left to play), Alfie would recall that the club had Scotch whisky on sale in the bar which, at a time when it was not widely available, was a bonus for everyone!

The Curtis Cup Series, which had started in 1932 and been suspended due to the war, resumed in 1948 after a 10-year break. Alfie and the boys caddied in the tournament where the British ladies were beaten by a 6.5 to 2.5 margin, and it is reputed that dropping local hero Frances Stephens from the British team cost them valuable points. A high point of the match was when Louise Suggs, the American champion, climaxed an uphill battle by winning the final two holes to halve her match (thus all square) with Philomena Garvey.

Alfie and Pat married in June 1948 and Alf borrowed a car from a friend so they could honeymoon in Blackpool for the week. They began a marriage based on love and trust. Pat got pregnant soon after the honeymoon, eldest son Mick being born the following year.

The war had been over for three years now and England was becoming a safer more stable place to live in. The late forties and early fifties saw golf becoming a lucrative sport with many top American golfers coming over for the big competitions. Naturally these were played all over the country, but Alf and the boys couldn't afford to travel so had to content themselves with looking forward to caddying in local competitions until another big tournament was held at Royal Birkdale. Alfie continued to dream of 'winning' an Open and in the meantime worked on building sites. Men who worked the building sites were called 'jobbers', but Alf wasn't only a jobber - he could turn his hand to many things. In the winter, however, work on the sites was often stopped because bricklayers and plasterers can't work in the frost. In order to bring in a regular wage, he took a job at the local sweet factory, driving the van and delivering boxes of sweets to outlets all over the country.

By the early fifties, Alf was travelling regularly around the country, but it didn't suit him or his lifestyle. He was contented in his marriage so he stayed with the job until the following spring when he put an advert in the local paper advertising himself as 'Alfie Fyles, local jobber'. He worked throughout the week to pay the bills and to earn enough money to get him to more distant tournaments at the weekends where he tried to make a go of caddying; he was now considering his yardages as a valuable tool.

Alfie's first four or five years were only moderately successful until he was paired up in 1951 with a young amateur Scottish player at the Walker Cup at Royal Birkdale. The young man played extremely well and Alf was delighted for him. Alf was totally hooked on the cut and thrust of the game and the prestige the success brought both the player and caddy alike. From then on, he went to every tournament he could possibly make, as did many of the other caddies including, Albert, Bobby and Teddy.

Albert Fyles and Teddy Halsall had both started caddying regularly in 1948 and when 10-year-old Bobby leigh started caddying the following year, the others took him under their wing, coaching him and watching out for him. The other children from Suffolk Road were, generally, good friends, but the four had a special bond which would become entrenched in their joint success over the years.

There would normally be two days' practice before the main match and the potential caddies would get to the course at the start of those two days and stand in line with the other hopefuls, waiting to be chosen.

"Who has experience of working with a professional?"

A sea of hands went up.

"You, son, who have you caddied for?"

"Sam Snead, sir."

"You?"

"Herman Keiser."

"You?"

It went on - very often they were names they had only heard of, but they were young and desperate to work so the truth was sometimes stretched to secure a job. Frequently, to secure a bag, more than one fact was distorted regarding exactly who they had and had not caddied for in the past. Alf being an excellent caddy, although he stood in line with the others, didn't have to wait long before his reputation preceded him and the players started ringing him up to see if he was available rather than his needing to stand in line on every occasion.

On November 11th 1951, Captain H F Simpson posted the following notice at the club:

'I have the honour to announce that His Majesty the King has been graciously pleased to command that the Club shall henceforth be known as The Royal Birkdale Golf Club.'

It was not only an honour but an accolade to the growing status of the club and it would facilitate Royal Birkdale becoming one of the finest establishments in the golfing world.

5

Beginnings of Success

Following on from his success in 1951 at the Walker Cup, Alfie was called to caddy for an unspecified player at the Penfold Tournament in 1953, when the competition was played at the Maesdu Golf Club. With Alf's support the golfer did well.

This incident changed Alfie's life and career expectations, spurring on his ambition to become a professional caddy. When he returned home, he couldn't wait to tell people all about it. After speaking to Pat, he made his way to his parents' house.

"God, Dad, you should have seen my man's face. It was a picture." Alfie highlighted the minutia of each hole and Ted was delighted for him. Margaret was equally thrilled and would share his story with many a neighbour over a cup of tea in the front room of their home. Alf went on to regale the story over and over to whoever would listen.

Alf's thirst to succeed as a professional caddy was a powerful motivation, but although he was keen to win, and caddied in every major event going, his ambition received little luck - until, that is, he met up with Gary Player in the early sixties.

Bobby Leigh left school in 1954 and immediately began general labouring as his regular job, caddying where he could. It is ironic that his introduction to big-time tournaments was also in this year - at the first Open to be held at Royal Birkdale. Although Peter Thomson won the match with a different caddy, (Peter would win the first and last of his five titles at Royal Birkdale) Peter and Bobby would go on to be paired up at St Andrews in 1957 and continue to enjoy a very successful and lucrative relationship on the course, remaining friends until Bobby died in 2004. In the meantime, Bobby had a good friend in Leeds who he caddied for and who found him work from time to time to eke out his wages, and in between he continued to labour on building sites when necessary.

The 1954 Open saw Teddy Halsall caddying for an unknown professional who, when he finished in the top thirty, gave Teddy £45, which was a great deal of money in those days. Teddy was terrified the other caddies would try to steal it from him and he ran all the way home with his winnings and gave it to his mother, who had never seen so much money in her life and couldn't conceal her delight. It was also around this time that, having caddied for many accomplished golfers, Teddy was paired up with Billy Casper who turned professional in the same year. Billy's father had taught him to play golf as a five-year-old, and Billy too started in the profession as a caddy but went on to become seventh on the all-time PGA Tour Champions list. Casper also won the Vardon Trophy for lowest scoring average five times in 1960, 1963, 1965, 1966, and 1968.

By the late fifties, many local Southport people worked on the fairground and/or Peter Pan's, including Alf, Albert, Teddy and Bobby, but Saturday evenings always saw the fairground workers hurriedly closing the rides so they could get home and change to go out on the town. Jazz and Bebop was giving way to skiffle and Rock 'n' Roll and the boys would go bopping in local dance halls. For Albert it was much more than a night out. In fact, if there was a bebop competition on, Albert would never miss it and would go to any length to compete. He won regularly, and by the late 50s was a much sought-after bachelor around Southport. Late one Saturday afternoon they were closing their rides when Teddy shouted over:

"Albert, you dancing tonight?"

"Is there a Y in the day? Course I am. There's a competition on at the Floral. Come on, you lot, get a move on, I need to go home and get ready."

He ran to the bus stop and let himself in through the back door. Margaret smiled as her son sang along with the Everly Brothers' 'Wake up little Susie' on the radio. She was proud of her children and both she and Ted remained close to them all, supporting them and fighting for them where they could. She felt particularly proud of Albert's accomplishments and was delighted that he had won so many dance competitions. He could have turned professional if he'd wanted, but he was happy with his life at the fair, his caddying career, and dancing in his spare time.

After his bath and with the towel tied around his waist, Albert Brylcreemed his hair and moulded it into a quiff. He then carefully slicked it back into a DA, as it was known, at the nape of his neck before dressing in his velvet-trimmed drape jacket and drainpipe trousers. A loose-collared white shirt, 'Slim Jim' tie and Brothel creepers completed the outfit. He was a fit young man and an excellent performer. Dizzy Gillespie played on the radio and Albert did a soft shuffle as he dressed.

"My God, son, what's that on your hair?" Ted teased. "What the hell are you wearing? Bend down and those trousers will cut you in half."

"Get with it, Dad, everyone is wearing this gear now. Don't be so square."

The light-hearted banter went on, and although he would never admit it, he too was proud of all his children and thought back to the days of freezing linoleum and not enough food to eat when he had foraged the courses for golf balls. Thank goodness, they didn't have to worry as his parents had, but still, the boys worked hard and their children were expected to contribute in their own way. Although they weren't well off, they didn't go hungry either.

As Albert got to the door Ted called out, "Don't come back unless you win."

Grinning, Albert half danced, half ran to the bus stop and

travelled into town, jumping off at the Monument stop just as a group of his mates were walking up Lord Street towards him. Many of them followed Albert, wallowing vicariously in his success and admiring his finesse, easy grace and professionalism.

One of the crowd wolf-whistled as Albert got off the bus.

"Hey, Albert, looking hot tonight, mate."

"Get lost, Pete, don't take the mickey." But his confidence was up and he put an extra bounce in his step as they walked the half mile to the Floral Hall where he met up with his regular dance partner Edna.

They won the competition by a mile and the whole crowd made their way across the promenade to celebrate in the popular Queen's Bar. This was their Saturday evening ritual, and wherever there was a competition, a huge crowd would accompany Albert and Edna to the dance hall.

Sundays saw the crowd at the popular Uncle Mac's Cafe on the promenade, where Southport's first skiffle group, the Steeldrivers, had a regular gig. They performed Lonnie Donegan songs, and Uncle Mac's was considered 'the place to go' at that time. Skiffle groups made use of anything they could to make musical instruments: washboards, tea chests and comb and paper kazoos - anything that would make a noise would do.

As previously stated, Southport had its fair share of characters and many of these worked on the fairground around that time, including the aforementioned Skid, who worked the bumper cars and earned himself the nickname because he would let the cars set off at about ten miles an hour, which felt much faster to the punters. When they set off, Skid would jump from one car to another to collect the shilling fare, and while the visitor, travelling at what felt like a hundred miles an hour, delved into his pocket to fish out the money, inevitably bringing out a handful of coins, at this point Skid would put his foot on the front wheel and the car would lurch forward, sending the money flying in all directions. When the customer tried to pick up the money, Skid would say, 'Oh don't worry, just give me a shilling, I'll pick that up for you later'. But of course, when he gave the money back, there was always half a crown missing.

Another character was Cadbury, who got his nickname because he never stopped eating. On a caddying trip to St Mellion, the breakfast at the hotel they were staying in had been set up continental style, which was very rare in Britain at the time. Cadbury came down before everyone else and saw the breakfast of eggs, bacon, mushrooms, sausages etc. laid out in bain marie dishes. The hotel was a guest house with twelve guests; all the breakfasts had been laid out so that each guest could help themselves to a hot breakfast, but when everyone else came down, Cadbury had scoffed the whole lot thinking it was all for him.

In 1957 the four friends were caddying all over the country, and that year they travelled up to Scotland to work at the Open at St Andrews. Everyone took their positions in the caddy line and, as previously said, Bobby was paired up with Peter Thomson, which began a long and successful career for both of them.

Thomson was drawn against Bobby Locke, and at the start of the tournament Locke opened with a 69, four shots better than Thomson's first-round of 73. They soon went head to head, with Locke maintaining the edge over Thomson throughout the game. Thomson cut three strokes off with a 69 of his own in the second round, and Locke regained two strokes with a 68 to Thomson's 70 in Round 3. However, he then forgot to move his marker back to its proper location before putting out himself. Apparently, the mistake wasn't noticed immediately but was reported later, whereupon the committee called for a Royal and Ancient decision as to whether the result could stand. The committee decided that with his three-shot lead and no advantage having been gained, 'The equity and spirit of the game dictated that he should not be disqualified'.

It was about this time that Alfie had an idea that raced around his brain. He wanted to write an autobiographical book based on his experiences. Unfortunately, he would never accomplish his dream, even though he gave it a great deal of thought over the coming years.

Peter Thomson and Bobby Leigh hit it off immediately, and in 1958, when Bobby was just nineteen, they paired up again for the Open at Lytham St Anne's, Thomson defeating Dave Thomas to win his fourth Open Championship title in a 36-hole playoff. Thomson had a 2-stroke lead after the third round, but Thomas shot 71 to Thomson's 73 in the final round to force a tie at 278. He took the lead in the morning, 68 to 69, then pulled clear in the afternoon, winning 139 to 143.

Besides caddying in many championships, Bobby became a good golfer in his own right and got a great deal of pleasure out of playing as well as caddying. For Bobby, just being on the golf course was a source of exhilaration, calm and tranquillity.

Peter and Bobby's seventeen-year professional relationship went much deeper than just employer and employee and Peter always called Bobby 'Jack'. When Bobby died in 2004, Peter wrote a moving eulogy to his favourite caddy (see chapter 10).

Unlike Alf and Bobby, who had always wanted a caddying career, Teddy and Albert had seen caddying as a way of making an extra few pounds or to help the family out. However, when Bobby had his success with Peter and got his name up in lights, they thought, 'Well, we can do that', and they too were encouraged to think about turning professional.

At the time, Teddy's loyalties were torn as he was working for a local furniture removal company. Then one day he said to himself, 'You know what? I'm wasting my time working for someone else. I'm going to get a van and run my own business'. Continuing to caddy part-time, he bought his own van, doing small removals for locals, and went on to start up his own business and buy a shop in Manchester Road, Southport, in the 70s. The company is still running to this day and has remained a family business throughout.

Pat became pregnant with their second child in 1958 and Alfie and Pat were delighted by the news. When Pat told her mother, Martha, and sister, Ellen, Martha cried out, "Oh, my God, I can't believe it." The three women looked from one to another, hugging each other, clinging on until they were crying.

Nine-year-old Mick walked in from school.

"Nana! Nana! Auntie Ellen." He flung himself into his grandmother's arms. She staggered back and fell on her bottom on the floor.

"Good gracious, Mikey, it's good to see you too!"

She went to get up but the room spun around her. Faltering, she swooned and leaned on the sofa to get up. Pat rushed over.

"You Ok, Mum? What's up?"

"Oh, just went a bit dizzy, Pat. I'm Ok, don't you worry yourself."

"Did you make that appointment with the doctor?"

"Don't fuss, love, it's just my palpitations. I'm OK. Nothing a fag won't put right. I'm just going out the back. I won't smoke in the house, not if you're in the family way." She chuckled as she made her way unsteadily to the back yard, ecstatic that she was going to be a grandmother again.

"Pat, you've got to make her go and see the quack."

"I know, Ellen, but you know she's a stubborn old bugger. If she doesn't want to there's no way anyone can make her."

Pat decided she would try again to persuade her mother to go to the doctor when the three of them went shopping for baby and maternity clothes. It was nine years since Mick had been born and Pat and Alfie had given up any hope of having another baby, so, having nothing from her previous pregnancy, she had to start from scratch.

While they were out Pat broached the subject of Martha seeing the GP but it was met with the same dismissal. Although worried about her, she and Ellen realised that nagging their mother would bring more and more resistance so they thought it best to leave it for another day. Chipping away might just help her to make a final decision.

Martha continued to be as supportive as always. She looked forward to seeing her next grandchild and considered that if she ignored her health problems, they didn't exist.

When Pat was 26 weeks pregnant she had a show, and had to go into hospital because the doctor was afraid she might lose the baby. There was no doubt that her mother would look after Mick. It wasn't a chore; she doted on her youngest grandson and had him to stay whenever she could.

"What do you want for breakfast, Mikey?"

"What ya got, Nana?"

"You can have toast, cornflakes or porridge."

"Can I have a piece of toast and some cornflakes please, Nana?"

"Go on then, seeing as you ask so nicely."

She reached up to take down the packet. The room swam and she gasped for breath. Gripping on to the side of the worktop she couldn't focus on anything but the pain in her chest. Mick rushed over.

"Nana! Nana, what's up?"

"Phone … phone …"

Mick knew what to do in an emergency. He ran to the phone

box and dialled 999. He told the operator what the problem was and coincidentally Alfie walked up to the house as the ambulance got there.

"Mick?"

"Oh Dad, Nana isn't well. The man said she needs to go to hospital. I rang for them. Dad, I was so scared. What do you want me to do now?"

Alf took Mick to a friend's house so he could go to the hospital. He then called at Ellen's house and they walked the couple of miles to the hospital. They explained to the ward sister who they were and she let them in immediately.

"The rest of the relatives should be here, Mr Fyles, this lady is extremely ill and we don't know how long she will last."

Alf felt physically sick. His mother-in-law had been a great source of support for both him and Pat and although he joked about her being a dragon he had a great deal of time for her. Pat, Ellen, and young Mike worshipped the ground she walked on and now, here she was, critically ill. The irony was that she was fighting for her life while Pat was desperately trying not to give birth in the adjoining maternity wing.

Alf and Ellen discussed visiting and realised that one of them had to go and see Martha while the other visited Pat, who would worry if she saw neither of them. They thought it best if he went to see Pat and Ellen stayed with her mother. They could change over for the subsequent visiting times.

Alfie called in at the WRVS shop and bought some tissues and Pat's favourite magazine. He joined the throng of visitors who were waiting to go into the maternity ward, steeling himself and taking a big lungful of air as he walked through the doors. He put on a smile that belied his true feelings as he leaned over and kissed his wife on the cheek. Pat was also suffering with a chronic back condition, and while she was in hospital had a period in traction even though she was pregnant.

"Hi, love. How are you feeling? Have you had any more shows? How's the back?"

They chatted about what the doctor had said and what the woman in the end bed had said and who had had their babies and gone home. All the time his head spun as he fought with his conscience about whether to tell her about her mother. He wanted to scream out that she had to go with him immediately to see her, but he knew the stress could make her condition worse and bring on labour.

If his mother-in-law survived, it wouldn't matter, but if he told Pat and she had a miscarriage, he would never forgive himself.

Racked with guilt he left at the end of the hour and went back to the main ward. He found Martha in a side ward, lying very still with an oxygen mask over her face. Her breathing was spasmodic and she was hooked up to all kinds of machines. Ellen talked to her nonsensically, pleading with her not to leave them alone. Alf looked at her pale, drawn face, blue tinged lips and yellowish skin. The machines bleeped regularly and the clock on the wall ticked as though marking out the final minutes of her life. He was uncomfortable in hospitals but went over and took her hand. He stroked it gently and told her everything would be Ok. At one point her eyelids fluttered and she seemed to respond to him, but the moment was soon gone and she fell back into an uneasy slumber.

"How is she doing, Ellen?"

"Not good, Alfie, she's in and out of consciousness. They are saying if she sees the next twelve hours out she might have a chance. Apparently, she had a pulmonary thrombosis which had caused her collapse. She's been having symptoms for months but she wouldn't listen to Pat and me when we wanted her to go to the doctor's."

They talked about whether they should tell Pat and agreed that for the time being it would be best to keep quiet and hope her mother pulled through.

Alf made his way back to his friend's house to see Mick, who wanted to know everything about his Mum and his Nana. He asked question after question but Alf didn't have all the answers.

"Can I go and see them tonight, Dad?"

"Not yet, Mick, they need to rest." If he saw the state of Martha and the machines and mask he would have nightmares for years.

The friend agreed to keep Mick with him until Alf got back after visiting. He went home and picked up a few things Pat had asked for and trudged back, calling in at the main ward so Ellen could go and visit her sister.

He settled in the chair, taking her hand and squeezing it.

"Come on, you silly old beggar. Your Patsy needs you. The kids need you, and for God's sake I need you to keep going. Don't give up, love, don't give up."

"Where's Mum?" was the first thing Pat asked Ellen. "I thought she would be here tonight. I'll bet that bugger Alfie is taking advantage and going out, leaving her to babysit, isn't he? Just wait till I get my hands on him."

Ellen felt terrible lying to Pat. Like Alfie she wanted to tell Pat, but the bleeding had stopped and neither of them wanted to shock her.

They kept this up for two days, visiting each woman alternately, and/or taking turns to look after each other's children. They were exhausted and it showed in their faces.

"What the hell is going on, Alf? Why hasn't Mum been in and why haven't you brought Mick in to see me?"

"Your mum's not 100%, Pat. She's had another of her funny turns, but she sends her love and is looking forward to seeing you soon. Mick's fine, but I don't know whether he can cope with visiting a hospital ward. You just get yourself better and you can see them soon."

The reason he didn't want to take Mick in to see his mother was because he knew he would tell Pat the truth; best for now to keep them apart and continue assuaging Pat.

Back on the main ward, he went to pull up the chair and was about to sit down when the machines went wild and alarm bells sounded. He almost fell backwards and called out for the nurse as the crash team flung open the door.

"Outside!" the staff nurse barked and, stunned, he obeyed.

For what seemed like a lifetime he watched the door, praying that she would live, when eventually the house doctor walked out of the room.

"I am *so* sorry, Mr Fyles, but your mother-in-law was pronounced dead at …"

The rest was a blur. He couldn't take it in. His brain couldn't comprehend what the doctor was saying or that Pat wouldn't see her mother alive again. His despair gave way to anger which melted into panic. What would she say? He went through a gamut of feelings and emotions, but realised he had to get hold of Ellen as soon as possible. In blind panic, he sprinted the two miles to her house and gasping for breath he burst in the back door.

"Ellen, oh my God, Ellen."

"Pat?"

"No, love, your mum."

Her legs went to jelly and she crumpled to the floor.

"No. No, I don't think so, Alf. You must have it wrong. Are you sure? Did they tell you she was gone? What did they say?" Her voice got louder and more panicky. "Pat - oh my God, Alf. She doesn't even know Mum's been in hospital. She'll never forgive us."

Luckily Ellen's children were with her best friend so they didn't need to worry about finding someone to look after them while they went back to the hospital. Ellen asked if she could see her mother and was inconsolable as they made their way outside for a cigarette.

"Alfie, Alfie, Alfie, what are we going to do about Pat?"

"God knows, Ellen. She was spotting again yesterday and I

really don't think she could cope with this right now, she's not strong enough."

"For Christ's sake, we can't just leave her not knowing, Alf. We've got to tell her."

Alf said he would do it, and hoped he could find the courage to do so.

His dilemma was heightened by the fact that he still had to tell Mick that his beloved Nana had died and he wouldn't see her again. He tried to rationalise and put the events into perspective, but it felt as though he was looking at a slow-motion movie in which he was an emotional puppet. He went over what he would say to Pat.

'I'm sorry, but your mother died this afternoon.' 'Pat, your mum has passed away.' 'Now don't get upset, love, but I've got something to tell you.'

No words sounded right and when he met up with her that night the words just wouldn't come out.

"Alfie, what's the matter? You look awful."

He fobbed her off with some tale about not sleeping last night. He knew what he had to do but he just couldn't do it. Ellen couldn't visit and he told her that Ian, Ellen's eldest, was ill, and she didn't want to pass anything around the ward.

It transpired that Martha had been under the cardiac consultant for more than six months and he had advised her that the embolism could cause a fatal heart attack at any time. He wanted her to give up smoking and change her lifestyle, but she didn't take his advice. Like so many people she saw herself as invincible and thought the final blow would never be dealt. The medication lay untaken because it caused side effects which she wasn't prepared to put up with; neither Pat nor Ellen had known.

Arrangements were made, and each day Alfie could not find the words to tell Pat. He was terrified that the shock would exacerbate her condition and she would lose the baby. But three days before the funeral Alf realised he could no longer keep the secret. He explained to the ward sister and she arranged for a private room to be made available for them.

"Pat, love, there's something I need to tell you."

"I knew something was going on. For God's sake, Alf, don't piss me about. What's the problem? Have you put all your wages on the dogs or something?"

"Your mum, your mum ..."

"What about my mum, Alfie? Where is she? She's Ok, isn't she?" Pat's voice was getting higher by the minute. "*Please* tell me she's Ok, Alfie." The panic in her voice was tangible.

"Pat, love, you know I told you she wasn't so good last week? Well, she was taken into hospital."

"So? Get me out of here and take me to see her."

"God, Pat, I'm so sorry."

Uncomprehending she gazed at him for a moment.

"Are you telling me ...?" She looked at the ceiling. "No. No, you're wrong. You must have made a mistake. Now take me to the ward she's on and you'll find you're wrong. She was smiling and laughing when I left her to come in here." Panic rose in her throat and her heart was pumping wildly.

"Pat, love …"

"Alfie, I want to see my mother. Please let me see her. So, what time did she ….?"

"She died on Friday, love. I couldn't tell you in case you lost the baby."

"And what the sodding hell do you think this will do to me? Please, please, Alf, tell me that I didn't miss the chance to say goodbye to her. Please, Alf, please."

Panic, anger, desperation - she felt totally out of control and hated Alfie at that moment.

Although Alfie had thought he was doing the best for Pat, she never fully forgave him for hiding the truth, and it was the start of the breakdown of their marriage.

Pat came out of hospital for the funeral. They took a wheelchair for her because the consultant didn't want her standing for too long. Unfortunately, though, the shock of her mother's death plunged her into a deep depression and caused her to go into early labour.

Tiny John Fyles came into the world in 1959, 10 weeks premature and weighing just over one pound. His first few weeks were a battle for him to stay alive. On numerous occasions they nearly lost him, and Pat was paranoid that he would die. Coping with a new baby is stressful enough, but coping with such a dependent little mite when you are grieving over the loss of a loved one, especially in such horrendous circumstances, was almost unbearable, and it was then that Pat contracted angina. Her relationship with Alfie would never be the same again, and she began to contract illnesses that were almost certainly related to the shock and subsequent depression.

6

Into the Sixties

The 60s twisted in as England became more and more affluent, skiffle and rock 'n' roll slowly but surely giving way to popular music, with Liverpool, Manchester and Birmingham making their mark on the music scene. Numerous now-famous entertainers and groups played in Southport including the Beatles, the Rolling Stones, the Hollies, the Troggs and the Small Faces.

Many new cafes and nightclubs opened in and around the area, and the caddying buddies frequented them, either alone or with their respective girlfriends and wives. Albert continued with his dance career, and in Southport there were many popular new venues including Uncle Macs, the West End Club, and the Kingsway Club. The newly formed Macombo Club hosted many of the Merseybeat bands including the Beatles, Gerry & the Pacemakers, Billy J Kramer, Rory Storm and the Hurricanes etc. At the Mocombo it cost two shillings (ten new pence) for a bottle of pop on the first floor, a shilling for a bottle of pop on the second floor, and a shilling & sixpence if you went up to the top floor where the band was playing.

Although none of the four Birkdale Boys caddied for Arnold Palmer when he won the 1961 Open at Royal Birkdale, it is an interesting fact that he used a Wilson Staff ball which is smaller than the ones used today. It measured 1.62 inches around, smaller than today's standard regulation 1.68 inches, and although in 1932 the United States Golf Association set the specification for golf balls at a maximum allowed weight of 1.62 ounces and a minimum size of 1.68 inches, the Royal & Ancient did not. Taken from the amended Rules of Golf in 1920, the R&A had agreed on a maximum weight of 1.62 ounces and a minimum size of 1.62 inches in diameter. Naturally, the smaller ball would have less wind resistance and thus go further than its bigger counterpart.

Under the R&A rules, golfers had the choice of which ball to play, an option which certainly helped Palmer in the 1961 Open when, as was frequent with weather conditions at Birkdale, the competitors faced gale force winds and torrential rain. Palmer hit a series of gobblers and made some amazing shots which others would be hard pressed to realise, and which Henry Cotton would be quoted as praising Palmer for 'playing one of the greatest shots ever'.

Palmer, who famously missed wining the Open in 1960 when

he fell one stroke behind Kel Nagle, went on to win the 1961 tournament by one stroke over Dai Rees.

Interestingly, it appears that the controversy over the size and weight of the ball had begun in 1920 during an informal conference in Muirfield between the USGA and the R&A. A decision on its use was made when the British ball was disallowed in the 1974 Open. It was banned from *all* competition play in 1990 when the diameter for golf balls was set once and for all at 1.68 inches with a mass no more than 1.62 oz (45.93 grams).

Over the decade of its use, Alfie was forced to review his yardages according to which size of ball was being used - the smaller, lighter ball would affect the distance it could travel, whatever the weather.

Following the 1961 Open, extensive alterations and additions were made to the Birkdale clubhouse, and spectator walkways were carved out on the course by re-siting tees and re-fashioning holes.

The First Piccadilly Number One tournament was held at the Hillside and Southport & Ainsdale Golf Clubs in 1962 with a total prize money of £8,000 including a first prize of £2,000; this was the largest-ever sum for a British event at that time. The first two rounds were split between Hillside and S&A, one round being played on each course. It was the first important professional tournament in Britain to have a planned Sunday finish. Jack Nicklaus made his first professional appearance at this event;

despite a 79 in the first round he eventually finished 15 strokes behind the winner. The 1963 event was cancelled and replaced with the new Gevacolor Tournament with total prize money of £3,500.

Pat and Alfie's relationship could be described as something of a roller coaster. They were both loving people but had tempers that easily flared when they were together. Alf knew which of Pat's triggers to press and, following their split some years later, son John recalls that when he was a little older his dad would come to the house to see Pat, and an argument as often as not would ensue. His mother would say, "I don't know why you come around here, Alfie Fyles, you only use me and you never give me any money."

"Money? Money? Is that what you want? Well, here." And he would systematically empty his pockets as he went around the house and leave it in piles just to prove a point.

John remembers coming down as a child and there would be piles of money sitting untouched on the table, window sills, mantelpiece and so on. Both Pat and Alfie agreed that, although they loved each other dearly, the fire in their temperament made it impossible to live together.

In 1963 Alfie teamed up with Gary Player at Lytham St Anne's, and although Player didn't win he tied 8th with Walter Burkemo. By now, Gary Player, Arnold Palmer and Jack Nicklaus were three of the most famous players in the sport of golf and played in tournaments all over the world, consistently spotlighted by the media. Everyone knew who they were and, in the twelve years Alf was with Player, he went to five Match Play finals at Wentworth, winning four out of the five. Alfie too became well-known both locally and in the wider golfing fraternity. The prestige of being a winning caddy, the elation of receiving the prize money, and the fame that accompanied it all went to Alfie's head somewhat, and although he didn't play around, he was a genuinely charming and friendly man who would go on to be pursued by the media and appear alongside his 'man' on TV and in the papers for years to come.

Gary Player earned the nickname 'Black Knight' from the media because of his penchant for wearing black clothing on and off the golf course, and for his courteous manner. This reputation stuck to Player for many years and became a keynote for his future business ventures, these businesses thriving to date.

Apart from Bobby, who travelled all over the world with Greg Norman and occasionally with Peter Thomson, Teddy was the only one who regularly caddied far afield. If there were any jobs going the four would be the first to know, and although they travelled all over Great Britain, and Alf once went to America, caddying at Pebble Beach, neither he nor Albert enjoyed being away from home, Alfie maintaining that he preferred links courses and they didn't have them abroad.

As said, Teddy Halsall caddied worldwide and you never knew where Bobby Leigh was - he could be anywhere, and following his success with Thomson he caddied for some of the most famous golfers in the world. However, no matter where the tournament was held, it would frequently be followed by lively parties. Successful caddies mixed with a lot of powerful and wealthy people; many relationships were formed, especially when the wine was flowing and the tongue was loosened.

In 1964 Alfie was attending an after-match celebration when he was introduced by one of the professionals to a well-dressed woman about the same age as him. They sat chatting and drinking and by two o'clock in the morning they were both talking the nonsense of partygoers everywhere: but they made sense to each other. By four they understood each other perfectly and had put the world to rights. By six they had shared a depth of understanding that can only be appreciated by anyone who has ever sat outside watching the sun come up after a night's celebrations.

Neither of them wanted to go to bed. Neither wanted to leave the other and go back to stark reality. But they both had responsibilities and realised that to leave each other was indeed what they had to do. They made no plans to see each other again and Alfie had no intention of doing so, but it was a wrench going home and Alfie thought about her often.

In 1965 the Ryder Cup was held at Royal Birkdale for the first time, during an Indian summer which would be remembered for many years. As was usual, the singles matches were won convincingly by the Americans. By the end of Friday, the home team were in with a chance, and there was very little in it when Boros and Palmer went head to head in the final round. Palmer's shot to the 18th was memorable, the pin positioned behind the left-hand bunker, but Palmer, undaunted, hit the ball with a 3 wood with the perfect amount of draw to get it to within four feet, and at the end of the day the crowds left disappointed.

Also in 1965 Gary Player won the Piccadilly World Match Play at Wentworth over Peter Thomson, and Thomson won the Open at Birkdale caddied by Bobby Leigh. Following the match, everyone was invited to the after-tournament party and Alfie, although he hadn't caddied for Player, was sitting in the corner discussing the finer points of caddying with one of his caddy colleagues. As he looked up towards the door, Margaret, the woman from the party the previous year, with whom he had felt such rapport, walked in, linking arms with one of the lesser known but up and coming professionals.

Alfie felt passion he couldn't understand or deny. It had been ten months since he had seen her and although he had thought about her since their initial meeting, he had not dwelled on those thoughts or feelings, dismissing them almost as soon as they came into his mind. He carried on talking to his colleague, but couldn't concentrate on the conversation. He kept making totally inappropriate contributions until his friend said, "You Ok, Alfie? You don't seem your usual self."

"I'm fine, thanks, mate. I was just thinking about that shot on the sixth hole today. Maybe I should have advised my man ..." But he didn't finish his sentence as he and his mystery lady caught each other's eye across the room and it took him off his guard. "Should have told him ..." He felt himself glow as she held his gaze for a moment. "Should have … sorry, Frank, I need to go outside a minute. Just had a bit too much to drink, I think."

It was a lame excuse but he stumbled his way through the crowd to the open door. The room had been stuffy and he drew in great lungfuls of fresh air, shaking his head and trying to make sense of his feelings.

He loved Pat, but since she had lost her mother and had contracted angina after having the baby, their relationship had changed. Even though they loved each other, her depression, both from post-natal causes and from not being able to grieve properly for her mother, meant she was no longer interested in a physical relationship with Alfie, and there were times he just didn't know how to cope with her physical and mental condition. He frittered away his prize money almost as soon as he was given it, and Pat found it hard understand the man he was becoming. He longed for someone to hold, but in all this time he hadn't looked at another woman.

His relationship with Margaret was different. For some reason this woman had got under his skin, and he was beginning to grasp the potential that a liaison with her could have.

Just as he thought he would leave the party, he felt a presence behind him.

"Hello, Alfie. I thought you were trying to hide from me." Her voice gave him goose pimples and again, he felt a bitter-sweet stirring in his loins.

"Of course not, why would I do that?" His voice faltered slightly and he forced himself to get to grips with his emotions.

"I don't know. I thought perhaps I'd made a fool of myself last year."

Oh, my lord! She was blaming herself for their not having met up since the last time!

"Good God, no," he stuttered. "I really enjoyed our conversation." Conversation? *Conversation?* What the hell was he saying? "What I mean is … well, you know … I enjoyed talking to you … being with you. Oh hell, do you want a drink and we can start over again?"

They sat as before, but by the morning they knew they wanted each other. The problem was, as well as having two children, he loved Pat more than he could ever imagine loving any other woman, despite their frequent ups and downs. Alf was a decent man and didn't want to be disloyal to her. Pat had stuck by him when he had nothing and always kept him together when he felt low or had a crisis. They had been through so many bad - and good - times together, he wasn't about to throw that way.

They talked once more, but more soberly this time. The drinks sat on the table untouched as they discussed their pasts and the things they had in common. It was surprising how much they *did* have in common and when they left each other in the early hours they had agreed that, although they felt a mutual attraction, they would not do anything about it. They would remain friends, and if they came across each other at similar gatherings they would take up the thread of conversation and carry on without getting involved. But of course, neither of them reckoned on the power of attraction.

Margaret lived in Parbold, approximately 15 miles from Southport, and before the end of the month they had met up at another social event which was held in the afternoon. The meeting was awkward with neither of them quite understanding what was expected of them. They tried to keep the conversation light-hearted and generic, but the problem was that they also found each other extremely interesting. The more they engaged in superficial discourse, the more attracted they became.

At the end of the function Alf asked if she would like to go on somewhere else.

"Why not come back to my place? I'm sure two friends can enjoy a coffee together, can't they?"

They both knew this wasn't the case, of course, but by now it was academic. By the time the taxi had arrived at her home they were burning for each other and only just held off kissing until they got inside the house. Alf had never felt this way before and the passion he felt for her was akin to being hit by an express train.

It was a relationship that would endure on and off for years; she asked him many times to move in with her, but he never succumbed. At one point Alfie said he couldn't because he had a young child to think of and commitments to Pat. She said he could bring John with him, but Alfie still said no. His two relationships were very different, but completely intertwined, and although he and Pat were apart they remained good friends, and there was just no way he would do anything that would cause her to feel abandoned. He would have given Pat anything and Ellen, his sister-in-law, used to say, 'You're too damned soft with her, Alfie.'

To which he would reply, 'You know what, Ellen? If I could take the stars and moon out of the sky for her, I would do.'

When Pat and Alfie finally decided that they could no longer live together, it hit Pat hard. She got herself a job and would cycle there and to school and back with tiny Johnny on a child seat behind her. She cried often and lost a great deal of weight, but as said, she couldn't understand Alfie's mindset or why he would give his money and belongings to his fair-weather friends. He would often come home broke because he had spent his money on others or had gambled it away. They argued regularly and Alfie would walk out, on Pat's orders, but he would use his infinite charm on her and soon he would be back home again. This continued until neither of them could tolerate it any longer.

Thursday October 6th 1966 saw Alfie preparing to caddy for Gary Player when he defeated Jack Nicklaus 6 & 4 in the Piccadilly World Match Play at Wentworth. Player won the tournament for the second successive year; the prize money was £5,000.

The first semi-final was even, both Player and Arnold Palmer not playing their best on the 17th. Palmer halved the hole in 6 to give Player a 2 & 1 win. In the second semi-final Jack Nicklaus was 6 up against Bill Casper at lunch. Casper won the 5th, 6th, 8th and 9th in the afternoon, reducing the gap to two holes. A birdie by Casper at the 16th reduced the lead to one hole, but Nicklaus hit a 1 iron to 12 feet at the 17th to secure a 2 & 1 victory.

In the final, Nicklaus drove poorly at the 17th and 18th and Player was on a four-hole lead at lunch. The match finished at the

13th hole in the afternoon after Nicklaus again got into trouble off the tee. There was a memorable incident between Nicklaus and referee Tony Duncan on the 9th when Duncan made a controversial decision on a stroke played by Nicklaus that ended in his landing in the ditch near an out of bounds area. Nicklaus dropped out of the ditch under a penalty of one stroke; he then maintained that an advertising sign about 50 yards ahead was in his line of sight, and claimed relief. Duncan decided that the sign was not in a direct line between ball and pin and refused to allow a free drop. Protestations from Nicklaus resulted in Duncan offering to stand down as referee; he was replaced by Gerald Micklem.

In 1967 while caddying for Gary Player in the Piccadilly World Match Play, Alfie met Gay Brewer for the first time and would go on to caddy for him later in the year.

While Alfie caddied for Gary, Bobby Leigh caddied for Peter Thomson. Alf always said that, just as the two golfers were formidable opponents and two of the best professional golfers in the world, he, Alfie and Bobby were two of the best caddies in the world and always jockeyed against each other to prove it.

On the first day Player, who had won in the previous two Match Plays, didn't play as well as he could, unlike Thomson who was on top form, so Player was taken to the 39th hole by Brewer in the opening round.

At the third extra hole, Player noticed that the green staff had moved the hole in preparation for the next day. He objected, and the referee agreed to replace the hole in its original position. However, there were no green staff available so they used a penknife to cut out the hole. Brewer's second shot had landed in a bunker but he came out 18 feet past the hole and three-putted to give Player the victory.

Many people still agree that the semi-final in which Gary Player and Peter Thomson went head to head was one of the most memorable for many years to come. Bobby would recall the fact that they ended up 3 down after 9, and after some very mediocre golf he was still 3 down at the 13th, but he chipped and putted superbly to get it back to 1 down at 15. Then he got an eagle to pull it back to all-square. Peter went 1 up with a great putt with two to play. Gary then put his out of bounds and was beaten 2 & 1, but all in all it was a great match.

In the final, Peter Thomson was 3 up over Arnold Palmer after six holes, but by lunchtime the match was level and remained so after 27 holes. Palmer took the lead with a birdie at the 10th and the game turned into one of cat and mouse. Thomson was unable to regain the lead and Palmer defeated Peter to win for the second time.

On the first day that Alfie caddied for Gay Brewer, he approached Alfie saying, "I believe you are going to caddy for me."

"I am sir, yes."

"I won't tolerate swearing or blaspheming, but anything else I can put up with. If I'm doing anything wrong, tell me."

Gay repeatedly talked to Alfie about his family. It was obvious he was devoted to them and Alf thought, 'My God, the hardest part of caddying for this man will be keeping his mind off his family while keeping him focused on his golf.'

Alf started chatting to Gay about the holes and what there was about that hole that was unique, keeping up constant distraction strategies. The tactics worked brilliantly and, when asked, Alfie said he considered they got on famously and that Gay was the finest golfer he had played with. Gay went on to become a member of the winning team in the Ryder Cup, which, as it was played in America, precluded Alfie from caddying for him.

When Alfie caddied for Gay at the Alcan Open, Gay reputedly won £55,000 and gave Alf his agreed wage for caddying. It was reported in a popular golfing magazine that Gay gave Alf a further £1,000 tip for being able to read the game and for knowing his art so well. There was some dispute over whether Gay had in fact given Alf such a large tip and he, Alf, vehemently denied it. However, because it had been written in the press, the Inland Revenue pursued Alf for many years to get their stake of the money from him. He eventually persuaded them he hadn't had the money, but it was touch and go for a while.

Gay told Alfie he would be back the following year and together they would win again.

Gay Brewer did indeed return in 1968 and he and Alfie won the Alcan again when the tournament was played at Royal Birkdale. Between visiting Britain twice, and competitions in America, he amassed prize money totalling over half a million pounds. He told Alfie it would keep him as his caddy for the rest of his life, but ironically from that time onward he didn't return to England. He invited Alfie to caddy for him in America, but Alfie didn't see his future over there, so that was the end of the partnership.

Alf's friend, John Murray (co-author of this book), who would go on to marry Alf's niece, Debbie, recalls the time when several of the men, including Bobby Leigh, were caddying in a local tournament at Formby Golf Club. John was the only one with a car and at lunch time they decided to go to the pub, which was a mile or so away. He ended up doing two trips to take everyone there and they all ordered a drink, except Cadbury, who ordered four pies to go.

It was the first-time John had met Bobby Leigh, but when they got back to the course, Bobby asked John, "How much do we owe you, Fyles's lad?"

"Nothing, Bobby, and I'm not Fyles's lad - my dad is over there." And John pointed to where his father stood with his 'man', waiting to go out for the afternoon's play.

"Aye you are - Alfie always says you are." From then on, Bobby only ever referred to John Murray as 'Fyles's lad', and in truth, Alfie was very much a father figure to John over the years. It was ironic that when John and Alf's niece married in 1985, effectively he became Alf's nephew.

In 1968, Player and Alfie went on to win the Open at

Carnoustie. Player was two off the lead entering the final round, as was Nicklaus. Billy Casper was the leader, with Bob Charles in second a stroke back but one ahead of both Player and Nicklaus. Casper lost the lead by the sixth hole, later regained a share of the lead but fell away again over the last third. He wound up shooting a final round 78 and finishing fourth.

Charles shot a 76 in the final round, tying for the lead on the first half of the back nine, but fell away later, leaving Player and Nicklaus level pegging. Despite Nicklaus shooting well, Player held it together and kept the lead. Player and Nicklaus both carded 73s in the final round, and Player won by two strokes over Nicklaus and Charles.

In September 1969, the Ryder Cup was held at Royal Birkdale with the bookies rating only a 4-1-against chance of Britain winning the tournament, but in fact it swung backwards and forwards in favour of both countries. On the final day, on the 17th, Tony Jacklin scored an eagle 3, which set up an exhilarating and thrilling final hole that resulted in a 16-16-point draw, the first draw in Ryder Cup history, and culminated in one of the most famous and memorable gestures of sportsmanship when Nicklaus conceded Jacklin's final controversial putt, although he realised a draw would ensue.

It was Nicklaus' first Ryder Cup and it is reputed that this began the lasting friendship between Nicklaus and Jacklin which would continue for over 40 years.

Naturally people made friendships and networked while on

the circuit. The caddies were no different and when Jack Nicklaus' caddie Jimmy Dickinson came over with him, he and Alfie befriended each other. Jimmy told Alfie that he had an excellent relationship with Jack, saying it wasn't a boss/worker situation and they were always close on the course.

Alfie said he understood and that he always felt he knew exactly how his own man was feeling, telling Jimmy, 'If I can look at him and realise when he's not feeling too sure here, or am able to know if he isn't sure if it's a 5 or 6, or if he was thinking 6 and I was thinking 5, that might make the difference between hitting a good shot and a not-so-good shot.' He went on to say that he and his man were not a partnership, they were one. He followed on with, 'If I can be of any help to him so he can feel better, I will do it. In a way, a caddy is like a psychologist and sometimes it's just about giving a nod or a wink in the right place to reassure him'.

Jimmy asked Alfie what he put his expertise down to, and he said it wasn't down to him being able to play golf (he didn't play), it was his being able to tell his man exactly how far he had to hit the ball, what he's got to carry and any dangers he needed to be aware of, then leaving him to decide how to do it.

Jimmy asked how he managed all that, to which Alfie replied that he went out first thing in the morning to see where the pin positions were on the green. He told him about his now-invaluable yardage charts and that he had taught himself to walk so his pace was as near as possible to a yard with every step he took. He said, 'Sometimes I'm in danger of getting in front of my man, but that is something I will never do. I always make sure I keep a few yards behind him because he's the main man. When he goes towards the ball, I am still counting how many yards he's got to the green'.

Jimmy said he did a similar thing, but he did it by eye. He said he could gauge distances like that, but he could see that what Alfie said made a lot of sense. Between the two of them they agreed that the best way to give help to their man was to give him confidence by knowing how far he was from the pin to the edge of the green. 'Say, for example, that it's 210 yards and by now I know that the pin is on the green by 12 yards and you've then got 12 yards to play whether you carry the full distance or whether you're going to float the ball in and let it roll a bit. But if you *are* thinking of floating the ball in and letting it roll on, you have a bunker on the left-hand side so you are better 10 yards past the pin than landing in the bunker. And that has worked for every golfer I have ever caddied for!

'If I give them the yardage, the onus is on them to play that shot. But at the same time, I am the first person to be sympathetic or to find an excuse. It won't matter what excuse, any will do, however lame. I say something like, 'You just got ahead of the ball a little' - whatever, just so he doesn't lose his confidence.'

Jimmy and Alfie got together and worked on this. Alf was the first caddy to be allowed to go out first thing in the morning. It seemed as if he was just going to look at the position of the pin, but he was doing much more than that. He was the first caddy to be given that information and it was given to him by the head green keeper every morning and he was expected to give it to the other caddies. The difference was that some were professional caddies and some of them were just bag carriers, so they used the information accordingly.

Alfie's yardages consisted of a rough map of the hole on which he drew a series of coded charts such as: BR Bunker on Right. Front 200yds. Back 200yds. He would take a marker and work out where the player should stand, what club he should use, how many shots it should take etc. For instance, if the ball was past the bunker he would only have to measure from the back of the bunker to the ball to know how far it was to the pin and therefore be able to advise the player which was the best club etc.

Some of the other caddies were picking up on this and Scotty from Glasgow watched Alfie, puzzled.

"How goes it, Alfie? What was you up to this morning, Alf?"

"Not bad, Scotty mate, but I'm working out my yardages."

"Ok, Alf. What are ye' yardages then?"

"Well, I want to find out how far it is to a certain position, so I find a marker on the course - doesn't matter what it is providing you can remember it - and pace out how many yards it is. Then I know how many yards it is to the green and therefore how many it will be to the pin. Then I know what club it's best to advise my man to use."

"My God, Alf, that's brilliant. I wish I had thought of that. Tell you what - I'm going to do that tomorrow."

The next morning saw Alf out early as usual. A while later Scotty appeared, pacing carefully, thinking deeply and counting earnestly. He relayed the information to his man, but the pro fell further and further behind. When he finished at the end of the day he was nowhere near getting on the leader board and gave Scotty hell for misleading him. Scotty met up with Alf, dejected and thoroughly fed up. Alfie asked what the matter was and he replied it had been a total waste of time. Alf was puzzled.

"It can't go wrong, Scotty, so what happened?"

"The damned bloke I used as a marker moved on. I'm sorry, Alf, but I think you'd better stop that stupid idea. My bag went ballistic and you're going to get into real trouble if you carry on."

Scotty and Alf had a good relationship and on more than one occasion Alf asked where the Glaswegian was staying when he was coming to Southport for a competition.

"Och, I don't know yet, I hav'nae booked anything."

"Why don't you stay with Pat, and I will be there as well? I know she won't mind. We can't see you sleeping in the green keeper's hut."

"Well, if you're sure, Alfie. I don't want to impose."

The arrangements were set and Alfie and Pat looked after him, making sure he didn't go short and providing him with a good breakfast. They had an evening meal in the local pub and when the tournament was over, Scotty went back to Glasgow with a fond 'Cheerio'.

Around this time, Alfie was living in Chestnut Street and a reporter from the *Liverpool Echo* visited Alf as he wanted to write an article. He suggested they take young son Johnny to the local playing fields on Portland Street to get some photographs. Pat went into proud mother state, fussing over him, wiping non-existent spots of dirt off his face and insisting he change into a clean, polo necked sweater that, being a small boy, he detested. Insist she did, however, and the three walked down to the fields.

A small crowd gathered to see what was happening. John stood as though he was going to hit the ball and Alf held up a pretend club to 'correct' John's swing. John hit the ball a fair pace and it landed perfectly inside a rabbit hole some distance off. A roar went up and Alfie declared with pride, 'I've taught him well, boys. See our future golfer'. The article was printed in the local paper but Pat, disillusioned by Alfie's increasingly infamous status, would turn to him and say, 'Ruddy well showing off again, Alfie. That's no way to influence the lad'.

7

Decade of the Duel in the Sun

In 1971 Teddy Halsall was introduced to Johnny Miller by Billy Casper at the 100th Open at Royal Birkdale. Teddy was 32 and Johnny was 22. In the golfing world, the name Teddy Halsall would go on to become synonymous with Johnny Miller.

Lee Trevino went on to win the tournament; it was a return visit for him as he had played in the 1968 Alcan at the club. Trevino had won the US Open twice before and also the Canadian Open in 1971. Trevino was apprehensive about winning the 100th at Birkdale but stormed it to gain a hat trick that year, winning over Lu Liang-Huan.

Trevino had a convincing win over Mr Lu, but third- and fourth-placed Tony Jacklin and Craig DeFoy were valiant contenders.

One incident singled the match out as particularly memorable when, on the 18th, Lu Liang-Huan accidentally drove into the crowd, hitting and concussing a female spectator. She was taken to the local A&E but didn't need to be admitted. It is reputed that three years later Mr Lu and the lady in mention met for the first time and Mrs Tipping and her husband were invited to Taiwan to holiday at the hotel owned by Mr Lu.

Mr Lu was a popular golfing celebrity and acknowledged the crowd's applause for his eagles and birdies with a polite tip of his hat, which, according to the local caddies, he had bought in the Pro shop on the previous day.

The 70s were exceptional times for the Birkdale Boys and amongst the major competitions they won, Alfie caddied for Gary Player in the 1971 Wentworth Match Play when he beat Jack Nicklaus; Lee Trevino won the Open at Muirfield, again beating Nicklaus and spoiling Nicklaus' dreams of achieving a hat trick (he had won the first two majors that year). Johnny Miller, caddied by Teddy Halsall, was close to winning, and Weiskopf finished 7th, eight shots behind Trevino. Finally, Tom Weiskopf won the Piccadilly World Match Play caddied by Albert, Lee Travino coming second. Albert would caddy for Tom Weiskopf for 26 years and also for Tom Kite, in which time they would win four major tournaments. Albert recalled that, while caddying on the pro-celebrity circuit, he also caddied for many famous people including USA president Gerald Ford, Bing Crosby and Bruce Forsythe.

As we have said, Alfie was generous to a fault, and when he

had high earnings he would treat people inordinately well and spend most of his money on others. Son John recalls the time Alfie took Pat and the boys to the Portland Hotel on Bedford Road; as he walked through the door he called out, 'Whiskey and cigars for all the gentlemen and wine and cigarettes for all the ladies'. He didn't care how much it cost him; if he was flush he treated people, even strangers, to whatever they wanted. From the Portland they went on to the Crown on Liverpool Road, and once more he bought everyone drinks and smokes. He then took the boys and Pat to the travelling fair which used to set up annually on the corner of Moss Road and Bentham's Way, and they went on whichever rides they wanted to. Money no object, they had an excellent night. However, John recalls, 'He must have spent £1,000 and he only had two drinks!'

In 1973 Teddy Halsall and Albert agreed to travel up to Troon together for the Open. Teddy was due to bag for Johnny Miller again and Albert was with Weiskopf. Teddy said it was one of the biggest and most memorable games of his career, not only because they ended up in the final but because of an incident that occurred with Albert, which nearly ended his game on the third day.

Alf said he would make his own way there and Scotty had insisted that, rather than stay at a B&B, Alfie should stay with them. 'Come and stay with Rose and me, Alfie. We don't have a great deal of space but what we have you are welcome to. I'll show you a good time and you won't want for anything'.

Alf arrived at Scotty's house the afternoon before the tournament. He was met by a barrage of noise. Alf came from a family of eight and was used to noise, but Scotty had thirteen children and only three bedrooms. The only place available for Alfie to sleep was on an armchair in the front room, but nevertheless it was free and warm and he was not ungrateful for Scotty's having reciprocated his and Pat's hospitality.

Teddy bought an old banger which cost him £92 including tax and insurance. Between them they had just £15 to last them for the week. But of course, they didn't have to worry about accommodation because they had a firm commitment to both professionals so had bed and board paid for them up front.

After opening rounds of 68 and 67 Weiskopf stayed clear of the field and Ted and Albert would dine out for years on the story of that Open. Teddy would recall, 'We were second to Weiskopf when the big fella equalled Palmer's 276 and didn't miss a putt. He finished three shots behind after once being two in front'.

Albert told the story from his perspective, enthralling friends and family with the tale of how they *almost* won that year. He also told of the way he nearly missed out on the competition. What happened was as follows:

By the end of the second day Weiskopf was on 135 and leading Miller by three strokes. Albert would later recall, 'I woke up on the third morning and couldn't get out of bed. I couldn't put any weight on my ankle and told Ted I would have to call in a substitute caddy'. It was no secret that Albert had, at this stage, put on more than a few pounds, which almost certainly added to the complications of a weak ankle. Gone was the lithe young teddy boy who won dance competitions in the 50s and 60s.

Ted replied, "For God's sake, man, this is the Open. You can win with Tom. Stop messing around and get your bloody shoes on."

"I'm telling you, Ted, I can't. It's too painful."

Teddy pushed Albert's feet into his shoes. "Look, mate, Tom and Johnny are paired up anyway. You carry the clubs and I'll help you where I can. I'm not going to let you give up at this stage. Lean on me." And that is what he did. Ted literally pulled Albert up the hills, giving him a hand down and holding the pins for Tom when he was putting.

There was no question of Ted not helping Albert. The boys had gone through so much together they were inseparable, and would move heaven and earth to support each other.

Tom continued to win with a 12 under par, and Johnny came joint-second with British-born Neil Coles with 9 under par. Teddy was proud that Tom and his best friend had won the Open and congratulated them both heartily.

Later, Tom told Albert that Ted was the only caddy besides Albert that he trusted to hold the pin for him since a previous caddy, a long time ago, had let him hit the pin. He later recalled, 'I made very few mistakes and nothing bothered me - which was unusual. I was at the top of my game and I was so confident, everything seemed in slow motion - my thinking, my preparations. It was my greatest memory in tournament golf'.

Gary and Alf didn't do so well and at the end of the

tournament Alf went back to Scotty's for the night. He sat himself down in the armchair and tried to sleep, but for most of the night there was bickering and shouting amongst the youngsters. Scotty and Rose shouted for them to be quiet and endeavoured to raise their voices over those of the children, but inevitably they didn't succeed.

At breakfast the next morning Alf asked what he owed Scottie and his wife for staying with him.

"Och, Alf. You don't owe us anything. Just get the kids a fish supper." Alfie paid up the money for a fish supper for the thirteen children, but in all honesty, he would have been better off booking into a hotel, never mind a B&B!

Amongst the many golfing characters of that period was Jimmy, who had moved from Liverpool to Southport in the 60s because he couldn't find work. The problem was that every time he succeeded in getting a job he got the sack for swearing. These days he would probably have been diagnosed with Tourette's Syndrome, but at the time he was just seen as a loudmouth who couldn't keep his tongue under control and who got himself in trouble every day of his life through his profanities. When he talked, his eyes would blink in rapid succession and his nose screwed up involuntarily.

Realising there was money to be earned in caddying, he decided to give it a go, but unfortunately, swearing was one of his better bad habits. He would also take charge of anything that he saw as potentially not being needed by another, then boast about his ill-procured gains to anyone who would listen. He smirked as he told a colleague, 'Well, my man said help yourself to my fags, so I did'. The fact that he had helped himself to all of them was beside the point. Jimmy saw it as fair game to take him literally and that was his mantra in life. He would take a golf ball out of the player's bag to keep in hand if he needed a provisional, but if he didn't need a provisional, the spare ball would go into Jimmy's pockets, and this way he would build up quite a satisfying stockpile.

On one occasion, two high-up officials in the American Central Intelligence Agency were playing in a tournament and, because Alf and the other three of the faithful quartet had become recognised and trusted caddies, many people who visited Royal Birkdale would ask for one or other of them by name. The other caddies knew that if they were in a pairs match going out with Alf, they would get a few shillings more than going out with an unknown. On this occasion, the professional recommended Alfie to one of the Americans as proficient and trustworthy, but unfortunately his colleague was being caddied by Jimmy.

As his man prepared to take a shot, Alfie noticed a stunning Rolex watch on his wrist and thought how expensive it must have been. As his man put his hand into his pocket after the shot, though, the watch had become loose and fallen off his wrist; neither Alf nor the player had noticed. They continued to play, and Alf and Jimmy were well paid for it.

As they came off the course at Birkdale, Alf pointed to the clock tower atop the clubhouse and said to Jimmy, "I don't know if you know it or not, Jimmy, but there's four sides to that clock and each one of them tells a different time."

Jimmy rolled up his sleeve and said, "It's ten past four, Alfie."

Alf was surprised that he owned a watch, much less the expensive one he had just checked.

"Must be a fake," he thought, but something tugged at the back of his mind - he knew something was wrong, but just couldn't put his finger on it.

That evening Alf went to the Mason's Arms, their local hostelry, and Jimmy was buying beer like it was going out of fashion, which was an unusual occurrence as he was usually broke. Alfie asked what was wrong with him as he had not stopped buying drinks all night. He knew Jimmy hadn't been paid enough to warrant being so generous and asked where he had got his money. Jimmy responded with,

"Mind your own effing business, you've had your ale."

Later in the evening, one of the locals told Alf he had bought a watch off Jimmy which turned out not only to be a genuine Rolex, but was solid gold and worth about £200 - a fortune at the time. Alf put two and two together and informed the man that he was certain Jimmy had procured it off one of the Americans while they had been out caddying for them that day.

Alf questioned Jimmy again. He said he had found the watch and, because it was on the floor, it was obviously meant for him. He said it was 'finder's keepers' but Alf told him he couldn't get away with it. He would enjoy his few pints, then people would talk, he would get caught for stealing the watch and his reputation would be shot, meaning he probably wouldn't be able to work at the club again. Alf said that if he returned the watch and gave it back to its owner, he would sort out the mess Jimmy had got himself into. He told both Jimmy and the man who had bought the watch that the people they had been caddying for were important guests and weren't to be messed with. The man handed over the watch and Jimmy reluctantly gave back to him as much money as he had left.

The next day, Alf went back to the Birkdale golf course and pretended to be looking for golf balls. He found a few, pocketed them and made sure he was seen, saying hello to some of the members as he walked around. One or two asked what he was doing on the course.

"Oh, just having a root around, killing a bit of time. I've got a job this afternoon and I'm just waiting till then."

Alfie then went in to see Bobby Halsall, the pro at that time, and asked if anyone had reported losing a watch. Bobby said no, he didn't think so, but he would ask around, and why was he asking. Alfie said he had found one on the course and it seemed to be a good one, but he didn't know if it was worth anything. Bobby made enquiries, but none of the members claimed the watch. Alfie told him to keep hold of it and if no one claimed it, he could give it back to Alfie after a reasonable period.

Two days later, Alfie went to the club to caddy and the pro called Alf over. He told him the American had phoned in and asked if his watch had been found. Alfie feigned surprise and Bobby told him the man had offered £100 reward for its return.

Alfie gave the local man who had bought the watch the difference between what he had paid and what he got back off Jimmy, and they had a drink with the rest.

Sometime later, Alf was caddy master at a course where a charity competition had been organised, the contestants in which were all ecumenical. Alf had invited various caddies to the match, but due to Jimmy's swearing, no one had told him about the competition. When he got wind of it, he rang Alfie to ask why he hadn't been called for a bag.

"Sorry, Jimmy, but you can't caddy in that competition. It's all churchgoers and you could really offend someone if you start your effing and jeffing."

"What're you talking about? I can hold my mouth if I need to. I can go for a few hours without swearing - oh come on, Alf. I'm broke. I really need the money."

Reluctantly, Alf gave in and arranged for Jimmy to caddy for one of the gentlemen on the day, but made sure that he, Alfie, was paired up with the gentleman's partner so he could keep an eye on him.

All was going well and Alf congratulated his man on a good shot. "Oh well done, sir. What a great drive."

Jimmy's man took his stroke and Jimmy jumped in with, "That's an effing well better one, your reverence. Well done."

On another occasion, Alf and Jimmy were caddying for two Japanese golfers and Jimmy's man hit his ball into the bushes. Both the golfers walked over to look for the ball, but it was impossible to find and they gave up trying. They walked back and the gentleman asked Jimmy for a new ball.

"Who the hell are you talking to?" he asked the man in a disdainful voice.

"You. You. You are my caddy."

"Oh no, I'm not," spat out Jimmy. "My man's got effing hair." And he pointed towards the bush where the man's wig swung gently in the breeze, still attached to the twig it had caught on as he retreated.

Alf raised his eyes heavenwards and groaned out loud.

Around this time a deep-rooted incident occurred, which led to an argument that so upset Alf that his brother Albert and he did not talk to each other for the rest of their lives. The cause of the argument was a well-kept family secret, which neither man would talk about. However, they both subsequently caddied in numerous tournaments which necessitated their being in each other's company, and it must have been hard to maintain professionalism when neither brother spoke to the other.

Another character, Billy 'Butcher' Lea, known to all as Butch, worked for British Rail and would spend his spare time caddying, socialising or 'gollying' (collecting lost balls and selling them to local shops or back to the players) just as many of the locals did. He would get the train from Southport to Hillside and walk back at the side of the rail track, 'walking the line' as it was affectionately known, looking for balls. Because the golfers and caddies were banned from going by the side of the track to collect lost balls, they had to incur the penalty and play on with a drop ball. Therefore, there were many hundreds of inaccessible balls just waiting to be 'found'. Butch would wear his British Rail uniform, and because he worked for the railway he was able to walk the line (although not of course legitimately, it being his own time). This way he would gather up hundreds of lost balls. He would then walk back along the other side and get back onto the train to return to Southport, pockets bulging with his ill-gotten gains.

On one occasion, he boarded the train with his side pockets bulging and his deep trouser pockets straining at the seams. He sat on the train and a lady looked down at his groin area, which was reminiscent of the Elephant Man.

"I can see you are curious, lady - golf balls."

"Oh, my goodness, that must be painful. I'm just recovering from tennis elbow."

Butch would take the balls home and grade them - anything with a cut or blemish would be given to the children, who would spend hours on the local playing field having a knockabout etc. However, any ball that was in good condition would be lovingly scrubbed and cleaned ready to take for sale. One Friday afternoon the insurance man called at the door and asked Butch's young daughter if he could speak to an adult.

"Dad! It's the insurance man," she called up to him.

"For God's sake, tell him to come back on Monday, you know I'm scrubbing my balls."

Fourteen-year-old Margaret's scarlet face was only one or two shades lighter than the visitor's and neither of them knew where to look.

Butch had a heeler dog called Rinty. He had had Rinty from a puppy and had taught him to find lost golf balls. When the dog was old enough to want to play, Butch would throw a golf ball into the garden - these days it would probably be called a wildlife sanctuary - in those days it was just an overgrown tangle of weeds, long grass and nettles. Butch would throw the ball and when the pup brought it back to him, he rewarded him with a dog biscuit. After a few weeks, when Rinty had become used to the game, he would hide a ball in the garden and pretend to throw a ball. This time, the dog had to work harder to find it and he would go sniffing and rooting, use his scenting skills to locate it; again, the treat would be a dog biscuit and he loved the game. After some time, he took Rinty with him to the golf course and pretended to throw a ball. The dog would race off, bring back a lost ball from the rough and sit wagging his tale, awaiting his treat. This would go on until they had walked an entire pathway and Butch ended up with his pockets full of golf balls to take home and clean up. He often visited the pub on the way home and many people recognised the little heeler as well as they did Butch.

In 1974 Alf caddied for Gary Player in the Open at Royal Lytham St Anne's. With opening rounds of 69 and 68, he established a five-shot lead over the field, headed by Peter Oosterhuis, Jack Nicklaus trailing by nine strokes.

High winds impacted on play in the early stages, but this was the year that the compulsory use of the 1.68-inch ball had been imposed and it is speculated that this added to the high scoring of the match.

The winds continued into the third day, which seemed to throw Gary somewhat and he slipped fractionally behind with a 75. Nicklaus produced a 70 but was still four shots behind Nicklaus and one behind Oosterhuis, who closed with a 73.

The final round saw Player shoot two birdies and an eagle in the opening six holes, but his 6 iron approach to the 17th pulled the ball left into the rough. However, a group of spectators waded in, finding the ball with just moments of the time limit left. The ball was deep into the rough, though, and Player only managed to move the ball six feet on his first attempt, but he came back and incurred just one dropped shot.

Now over-enthusiastic with his second shot, he finished close to the clubhouse wall behind the green. The only way to play the shot was left-handed, but he rallied to the challenge and won his third Open title with a score of 282, four shots clear of Oosterhuis, and Nicklaus a further stroke behind. He was delighted and asked Alf how much he owed him.

At this point, Alfie had liaised with some of the American caddies who were involved in a dispute in the States about agreeing a minimum fee which a caddy could expect for supporting a winning professional. Many caddies from the USA had been exploited and they had finally agreed on a fixed percentage of the professional golfer's winnings. Alf told Player that he would like this rate and it is reported that there was a dispute over what Gary would pay. Gary was known for his charitable work and he reportedly said that the amount Alf was asking was a higher percentage than he gave to his charities, so he wasn't giving that amount to him.

Alfie explained politely that what he was asking for was the accepted rate in England at that time. He pointed out that the golfer got the prestige and most of the money and the caddy should get the going rate. Gary refused, and Alf said if that was the case he would not be caddying for him the following year. Alf had caddied for Gary for many years but this was undoubtedly the end of an era.

There is a quote on Gary's website in which he states: *The act of charity really begins in the heart*. The website also revealed that, while walking up to the final hole at the 1962 US Open Championship, Gary turned to Joe Dey, at that time director of the United States Golf Association (USGA), and with disappointment said, 'Had I won, Joe, I planned on giving the prize money to charity. But let's keep that a secret. One day I shall win, and turn back the money to a good cause. That is a promise'.

That promise was fulfilled three years later at Bellerive Country Club in St Louis, after an 18-hole playoff with Australian Kel Nagle. Upon being handed the winner's cheque, Gary handed it back to Joe Dey, specifying that the proceeds should go to cancer research and the development of junior golf programs by the USGA, saying, 'There is enormous satisfaction to be derived from giving something back to the world in moments of success'.

Alfie's sister-in-law Ellen died in 1974, but what many people didn't realise was that she and Alf had an annual tradition of going to the George pub every Christmas Eve. They had an excellent friendship and although it was never based in romance, they shared some touching moments over the years.

Ellen would prepare everything for the children and lunch for the next day, then she would disappear to meet up for a Christmas drink - or two. Pat would never join them, although she knew she would be welcome, but she preferred to stay at home on her own. In previous years, she would have been listening to songs on the radio or playing her favourite records on the record player, but by 1974 she preferred to watch a good film or the midnight service on the TV.

Christmas Eve this year saw Alf standing at the bar, dejectedly nursing his pint of ale. The aptly entitled 'It'll be lonely this Christmas' played on the TV behind him and Alfie looked at the space at his side where Ellen should have been.

"Oh, Christ, Ellen. What am I going to do for a mate now?" Tears welled up in his eyes but he didn't bother to hide his pain as he raised his glass and looked up towards the ceiling. "God bless you, love, rest in peace and share a drink with the angels, just for me."

It was probably the barmaid collecting glasses, or it could have been part of the song, but he swore he could hear chinking and a 'Cheers, Alfie' rebound around the room.

At the 1975 Open at Carnoustie, Player brought his own caddy over for the Open so Alf was introduced as caddy for Tom Watson. Alfie said, 'I saw a fresh-faced kid from Kansas coming up the drive and I thought, 'He'll do, he's got winner written all over his face''.

This was Tom Watson's first Open and was also his first time playing on a links course. The normally wet and cold Scottish weather was unseasonably warm and there had been a dry summer which had made the fairways firm and fast with very little rough growing.

Play saw Watson hit a first round of 71, which left him three shots behind leader Bobby Cole and in the frame alongside Jack Nicklaus, Australian-born Jack Newton, Johnnie Miller, Hale Irwin and England's Peter Oosterhuis amongst others, nineteen players breaking the course par of 72.

On day two the weather had worsened and Tom carded a 72 for a two-round aggregate of 279 and then watched as, one by one, the other leaders failed to equalise, some of them moving backwards down the scoreboard. Nicklaus equalised Watson's 72 and when Miller failed to get out of a fairway bunker on the 72nd hole it was left to Newton to 2-putt to tie, necessitating an 18-hole play-off to decide the title - this was a cause of much discussion and speculation between Alf and Teddy when, later that evening, they debated what the result might have been if Miller had easily got out of the bunker.

Sunday saw the wind increase, producing higher scores. The play-off began with Watson gaining an early two-shot lead, but Newton quickly pulled even and went in front at the 12th. Watson responded with an eagle at the 14th and regained his lead. At the

18th the two again stood level. Watson was on the green in two while Newton put his second shot into a bunker on the left. He played out past the pin and it was settled when Watson too putted from 20 feet on the last, and the Australian missed from 5 feet. In the end, Watson recorded a 71, one better than Newton, to win the game. Teddy Halsall was caddying for Johnny Miller and Miller had it in the bag but threw it away. Ted always said he felt sick whenever he thought about it.

He recalled, 'We were with Watson and leading, with Tom a shot behind us on the 72nd tee. Johnnie stopped to speak to Tom and lost it right there. I believe if he hadn't spoken to Tom he would have won. He told Tom he was still in it. In speaking to him, it broke his concentration. He came to me on the tee and asked for his driver. I wanted him to hit the 3 wood because of the fairway bunker. I told him it would only be a 7 iron second, but he played the driver and though he hit a super shot he got a bad bounce into the bunker. When we got up there Johnny asked me what he needed. I said, 'You need four to win the Open'. When he left it in the bunker I've never felt so sick in my life'.

Ted went on to say, 'Johnny asked me what club it should be off the fairway. I said the 9, so it should be the 7 from the sand. I thought he'd taken the 7 but he hadn't. He'd taken the 6. He fell right off the shot and hit the lip of the bunker. It was horrible. Then with the same club he finds the edge of the green and almost sinks the chip!'

At the end of the tournament Tom asked Alfie how much he owed him and there was a dispute over how much he would pay.

It is reported that Alfie was disgusted with the cheque Tom gave him and threw it to the floor. He said he would not be caddying for Watson the following year, to which Watson replied it was up to him. Alf stuck to his word and didn't caddy for him the following year. Alf often relayed the story and would refer to the cheque as a Gregory Peck, as per the cockney rhyming slang he often used.

Bobby and Teddy were members of the town's Park Golf Club, which played on the municipal golf course, and at times they had taken the professionals they were paired with into the club. Bobby had introduced Peter Thomson to the club years earlier, but on this occasion, he had been to Manchester to work and brought back the young man he was caddying for.

One member, Jack, was affectionately known as 'Nasty Jack' because he didn't have a good word to say about anyone, and if he did, he wouldn't say it. Bobby sat at the table with the young man and on his way back from the bar Jack stopped and said,

"So, is this the new man, Bobby?"

"It is, Jack, yes."

"Well, let's have a look at you, lad."

The young man started to stand up and continued and continued until, at six-feet plus, he towered over Jack.

"You're not built for bloody golf, man. You're built for rugby. You'll never make a golfer while you have a hole in your arse, lad. What's your name, anyway?"

"Greg Norman, sir."

Around this time there was another character, 'a wee Scottish caddy' on the circuit, called Allistaire, nicknamed Alli, who was renowned for his abrupt nature. On this occasion, he was bagging for an American and it was obvious he didn't like the player. After three holes, he overtly looked at his watch and the player asked,

"Are we on time? Do we need to move on?"

"It's not a watch, sir," Alli retorted, "it's a compass."

They played on and the professional said, "I'll tell you what, Jock, I'm not overstruck on your golf course."

"We left the golf course ten minutes ago, sir," was Alli's acidic reply.

When they had finished, the player handed Alli his money and said, "I've got to be honest with you, Jock, you are probably the worst caddy in the world."

To which a straight-faced Alli replied drily, "Oh no, sir, that would be too much of a coincidence."

In 1976 Johnny Miller won the Open at Royal Birkdale with Teddy Halsall caddying. Ted said that Miller hardly put a foot wrong and although he initially went three behind, he won by six and, picking up nine shots in seventeen holes it all came together on the sixth. He said to Miller, 'It's 468yards, just under the maximum. If you get a four here, you will go on to win the competition'.

Teddy said Miller hit a drive and a 1 iron onto the green and got his four. They had a dispute on the eighth when Johnny wanted to use his driver but Teddy, knowing the course like the back of his hand, and realising there were hazards on all sides said,

'Look, you're hitting your 1 iron 260 yards, why not take that?' Miller did and hit a 5 iron for the second, getting another birdie. From that point, he trusted Teddy's judgement and said, 'OK, Ted, just give me the clubs'. He hit the 1 iron 42 times in that Open. Teddy said, 'That's local knowledge'.

The 1976 Open was played at Royal Birkdale and Alfie was upset because he particularly wanted to caddy for Tom Watson on his own ground because he knew it so well. Alf was down on his luck at this point and considered regenerating his idea for the book. The problem was that a lot of the information was in his head and not recorded anywhere. Alf told his friends that the people interested in his biography seemed more concerned about sensationalising his private life and his extra-marital relationships than his golfing story, so once more it went onto the back burner.

At the Open, Alfie caddied for the Japanese Norio Suzuki who came in the top 20. This was the first time the eastern countries had come anywhere near and it is reputed that by then Tom Watson had recognised that it was Alf's aid that had helped him do so well.

Whether it was for this reason or not, he got back in touch with Alf for the 1977 Open at Turnberry, saying he thought he might have made a mistake and asking if he would consider caddying for him again. Alf said, 'Yes, I would sir,' and told Tom that the day he arrived, he, Alfie, would be waiting for him.

Many years previously, Alf and Pat had bought a Zephyr car which the family nicknamed 'The Green Goddess' because she was so big and beautiful. He used this to go up to Scotland that year for the famous *Duel in the Sun* Open.

Alf arrived at Turnberry two days before the start of the tournament. He wanted to gauge the course and the yardages, look at the weather forecast, consider the hazards, and how the greens ran. He was out early each morning, walking the course and taking in all the aspects he needed to ensure Tom was as supported as he could be.

At the start of each round Alf was out before anyone else arrived. He had been given special permission to walk the course, then feedback any relevant information to the rest of the caddies; he was always accurate in relaying that information.

He made his way over to the pro's tent and talked to Tom about the course, motivating him and firming up details. Alf said that Tom had a perspicacity that many golfers lacked and Alf admired him, knowing they worked well together.

Years later, one of the younger caddies asked Alf which was the best tournament he had ever taken part in and Alf said it had to be the Duel in the Sun. He recalled,

"I got the chance to meet and shake hands with Henry Cotton, a legend to us all - it was brilliant, but it would turn out to be his last major championship, you know, and he was made a Knight Bachelor in 1988. Anyway, the four of us were there: Watson, Nicklaus, his caddy Angelo Argea and me. We were enjoying some beautiful weather and it was amazing. Even on day one you could see it was going to be a brilliant competition. Day two was pretty much the same as day one with Hubert Green joining the leaders, although not for long because bunker trouble caused him to drop back. Tom made a charge with some great golf shots to go into the lead, 4 under at the end of the day, soon to be joined by the 'Mighty Jack Nicklaus'.

"On Day Three I went out early as usual and reported back to the caddies. It was a beautiful day, even so early in the morning, and I thought the weather forecasters had got it wrong when they said it would rain. I went back to report to the others, but in all fairness, there wasn't much to tell - the course was pretty much as it had been on the previous days.

"The first few holes were Ok and when we reached the 6th green, Tom asked me what I thought. I said, 'Well, sir, you are two shots behind him and the putt won't be easy. You are going to have to play left to right, and with you being right-handed that's going to be a killer'. Tom putted perfectly, knowing that every shot was crucial. On the 7th he made a brilliant drive off the fairway for a par 5 which he made to look easy, and then he sank a twenty-footer on the 8th, but Jack kept his lead, not really bothered by Tom's skill."

Alfie pondered for a few moments, savouring the memories.

"As the day went on it got hotter and hotter and it was getting uncomfortably humid. Then just as Tom plays onto the green at the par 3, there's a flash of lightning and play is suspended. The four of us ran to the beach, a few hundred yards away, and we waited while there was the granddaddy of all thunderstorms. By the time it cleared, the duel was on and by the 9th the crowd was getting more and more excited as they realised that something very special was happening. Now I don't know exactly how it happened, but the guide ropes suddenly snapped and the crowd poured out onto the fairway. They were virtually uncontrollable and Jack refused to play on until the onlookers were safely back behind the rope. The four of us stood in silence because there was nothing to do but wait until the crowd had settled. After 15 minutes or so all was back to normal and they played on, but when we reached the 14th we had to wait again while another crowd passed over the crossroad in front of us. I remember Tom looking out towards the horizon and saying to Jack, 'This is what it's all about, isn't it?', to which he replied that it sure was'.

Alfie chuckled. "I kid you not, at that point, nobody else in the world existed. The golf is nip and tuck and the weather is now superb. We have two of the greatest golfers the world has ever seen going toe to toe in the most prestigious worldwide tournament. Life doesn't get much better than that. These two giants of golf have matched each other with day one 68 68, day two 70 70, and day three ended in a 65 65. Anyone who knows anything about golf would have swapped places with me right then and there. Right, so, things hot up and Jack sinks a gobbler on par 3 to go one up, but then Tom hits a brilliant drive off the fairway at the par 4. Tom gets his birdie to go 8 under and become joint leader with Jack. At the 9th Jack sinks his putt for par. Tom misses his, Jack goes one in front at the turn and by now the crowd are getting increasingly excited. In fact, Charlie Jack, David Logan and the other marshals are struggling to cope. Jack sinks another birdie to go two clear with six to play." Alf pauses for reflection and shakes his head.

"Next hole, Tom sinks his putt to go one behind. The next par three Tom hits a 4 iron just over the bunker, four foot off the green. Jack just makes the green. On the 14th, two good drives then Tom's 2nd goes six foot away, but he misses the putt. Two more easy pars and Tom's still one back. On the 16th he makes a superb putt off the fringe of the green to go level with Jack, ten under.

"At the 17th, Jack hits a massive drive but Tom finds the green quite comfortably. Jack misses short and right but chips up to four foot. Tom gets an easy par and Jack is left with a nasty four-footer and misses it on the left. Tom goes one ahead, 11 under on the 17th. At this point the crowd are becoming frenzied and moments of silence are interspersed with roars and cheers."

Alfie paused and thought back to his first caddying job and the Open he 'won' with Reg Brown. He smiled and was pressed to carry on.

He continued, "At the 18th Tom teed off with a 1 iron, hitting a great drive, but he was bothered about the bunker down on the left. Jack tries to cut the corner but pushes it out towards the gorse. Jack plays his second from two feet from the gorse, a brilliant strike onto the green. Tom asked me how did I think it lay and I told him he was safe. Tom was sweating, not only from the scorching heat but because he couldn't see the ball. Suddenly, there it was. Tom said to me, 'Oh no, Alf, he's going to make that putt.' I reassured him he was safe and told him he had 178 yards. Tom went to look at his ball. He took out a 7 iron. I nodded and Tom hit it squarely. The grass was heavy and he took a large divot out. With a hefty swing the ball tumbled out, bouncing short straight onto the green, 18 inches away from the pin. At that point, he knew he was close but didn't know exactly how close.

"I said to him, 'You've got it now, sir'. But Tom still wasn't convinced and thought that Jack would go on to win. The air was electric and all our hearts were beating like mad. The spectators are going wild and as we make our way to the green everyone is jockeying for best position. I get bustled to the ground and my watch gets broken. Tom came over to me and asked if I was OK. I was, but the watch was never the same again.

"On the green, it's Jack to go first and we watch with trepidation because we all know what Jack is capable of, and sure enough, even under all that pressure, he sinks it right bang in the middle. The crowds are cheering like mad, although Tom was about to take his shot and defiantly he thought he would finish now whether they were cheering or not. But Jack raises his hand and the deafening roar just stopped. Just like that - cacophony, then nothing. Tom swung his last shot and the ball went dead centre into the hole.

"Jack walked over to Tom and put his arm around his shoulders. The crowd were in ecstasy once more, shouting and screaming with joy. Tom thought Jack would break his neck he squeezed so tightly. The two chatted as they walked to the scorers' tent and, apparently, Jack told Tom he had given it his best shot, but it wasn't good enough. He congratulated Tom and they walked back to the clubhouse together."

Alf and Tom would work together for another nine years and

they won many more competitions including another three Opens.

Pat used to enjoy crochet and soon after Alfie started caddying for Tom Watson she made a poncho set with his children in mind. Pat asked Alf if he thought it would be appropriate to give it to him and was delighted when she received a thank-you letter.

It is reported that Tom sent Alfie a cheque for $500 each Christmas and that Linda, Tom's wife, also sent Pat an annual Christmas card enclosing a cheque as a present.

Around the late 70s, Teddy Halsall's furniture removal business was doing well and once more, he wrestled with the dilemma of working for himself or becoming a full-time caddy. He was successfully caddying for Johnny Miller, who asked him to accompany him to various competitions in America, but Teddy was concerned about leaving the business.

"Well, Ted, what do you say?"

"God only knows, Johnny. I've worked hard building up this business and I don't think I can just up and leave Southport."

"Think about it, Teddy. You can stay at home running the business and earn £2,000 or go and caddy for me for the same period and earn £5,000."

Johnny eventually subsidised the business and Ted did indeed take the opportunity to go over to America with him, leaving the business in the safe hands of his family.

As is obvious, for Alf, Albert, Bobby and Teddy, caddying was about much more than just carrying a bag of clubs around. They all had good relationships with the players they caddied for. Each one of them considered their success was not solely down to their pro's ability, it was also down to the fact that they had gained the knowledge to support them. They were mini psychologists, able to take a situation that was almost irretrievable and turn it around. This was exactly how it was with Tom Weiskopf and Albert, where their relationship was more akin to friendship than employer/employee.

Amongst the many caddying characters was a gentleman called Tuttie. Tuttie couldn't pronounce 'th' or 'ck'. When he wanted to order a drink for three people he would say, 'Two pints of mild and anudder one'.

Alfie always wore a hat, which he called his bonnet, no matter what sort of clothing he was wearing. He had a variety of hats and caps which he would wear on different occasions. One day he went into the Mason's Arms and met up with Tuttie while he was wearing his tam o' shanter.

"Eh, Alfie, I like your bonnet. Where did you buy it?"

"I got it from Rawcliffe's, Tuttie."

"Wouldn't mind one like dat, Alfie. "

"If you like, mate, I will go with you and I can make sure you get what you want. It's only around the corner - we can go now if you want."

"Tanks, mate. Dat's good of yer."

Tuttie and Alfie walked in the door of the shop which then was situated on the corner of London Street and Hoghton Street.

"And what can I do for you gentlemen this afternoon?" the young assistant asked politely.

"My friend would like a tam o' shanter like this one, please."

"And your size, sir?"

"I don't know, mate." Tuttie tried to sound macho but was intimidated by the assistant's presence.

"That's Ok, sir, I will just get my tape measure and we can establish your hat size. Hmm. Yes, six and seven-eighths, sir. I will bring you one to try on."

"Sits and even eighths? Futt off, mate. My neck measures 15. How the hell can my head measure less than that? He knows nutting, Alfie." After which he disappeared out of the door, round the corner and back into the Mason's Arms.

Alfie told friends that he caddied for Ken Brown, a famous golf broadcaster and writer who now commentates on the European Tour and at major tournaments including the Open.

Alf said that Ken was renowned for being a slow player, which contributed to his distinctive and unique style and resulted in many prestigious wins. However, Ken's sponsors asked if Alf could possibly speed up Ken's play, offering him a cash incentive if he could. Alf said that to speed up his play they would be taking away the essence of the man and he would lose his integral ability to win.

Alfie didn't only caddy for professionals. He loved the game and would go out with friends and amateurs if they asked. If there was a pro-am match he was always eager to pair up if appropriate and would be requested to caddy for many of the top celebrities.

In the 70s and early 80s Alf used to regularly caddy for comedian Tom O'Connor. On one occasion Tom was due to play at Wentworth and he offered Alfie a lift because he also lived in Southport and it meant Alfie would not need to use public transport. Tom arranged to pick Alfie up outside his house early on the morning of the tournament.

When Alfie walked outside to wait for Tom, the aforementioned Tourette's sufferer Jimmy was standing there waiting for him. It transpired he also was going to the tournament. He asked Alfie how he was getting there and Alf said he was getting a lift with Tom.

"Oh, all right, I'll come with you, then."

"I don't know, mate, you'll have to ask Tom if that's Ok. I can't say yes or no."

"Well, I will, I will," he said. "Effing hell."

"But if you do get a lift with us you'll have to watch your language. Tom won't want you effing and blinding. Ok?"

"What the effing hell do you mean?" he said.

Alf shook his head. "Just watch your language, Jimmy. That's all."

Tom drove up in his Jaguar and got out.

"All right, Alf? Hello, Jim, where are you going?"

"Well, I'm coming with you. I'm effing well coming with you, aren't I?"

"I don't know, are you?"

"Yeah."

"Oh, right, have you got a bag? Who are you caddying for?"

"That De Courcey fella. The nooky, nooky one."

"Oh, Ok, get in." But before they had even left Southport, Tom had stopped the car and turned in the driver's seat to look at Jimmy. "Jim, stop with the swearing."

As Tom drove off, a voice came from the back seat. "What the effs the matter with him, Alf?"

"THAT's what's up. You! That language."

"I haven't effing well done anything."

A patient Tom said, "Jimmy, I've told you once and that's enough. I've heard enough of you now. If you don't stop swearing I'll throw you out of the car."

Tom carried on and the two men discussed having seen Tom on television the night before. The conversation was going well when from the back seat came, "I hope you was better than that effing De Courcey. He's sh**e. I bet that effing Nooky bear is better than him."

Tom growled, "I've told you, Jim."

"What, what?" Silence for two minutes. "Effing hell."

Tom knew when he was beaten. He turned to Alfie and said, "Do you mind, Alf? I'm going to put the radio on *very* loud. You are welcome to join me on the return journey, but *he* is not coming back with *me*."

Jimmy's last shot was, "And I hope this De Courcey's golf's better than his effing ventriloquism."

Late in the 70s the boys were caddying at St Mellion in Somerset and had been up early. At lunchtime Alfie and Jimmy were taking a walk around the local town. They were due to go out again in the afternoon so had decided not to have a beer but see some of the local scenery.

There was a cortege coming along the street and Alf followed his usual routine of removing his cap and laying it against his chest, putting his hand flat over the cap and bowing his head.

Jimmy asked in his usual loquacious manner, "What the effs up with you? You don't effing know him."

"It doesn't matter whether I know him or not, I'm just showing a bit of respect, mate. All right?" and he bowed his head again.

A lady walked up and stopped by the side of them. Thinking they were locals she asked, "Who's dead, my dear?"

At which Jimmy piped up, "Him in the first effing car of course."

In 1978 Alfie became caddy master at Walton Heath, Surrey, and was caddying part-time. On this occasion, he was paired with Tom Watson, who was playing against Jack Nicklaus in the Open at St Andrews. Alfie could see he was in two minds about what to do next.

"Where are your thoughts, Tom?"

"A 4 iron I think, Alfie."

Alfie was thinking of a 5 iron and put his hand on top of the clubs saying, "The adrenaline's flowing, you are hitting the ball well. A 4 iron will put you through the back. Just take a few minutes to ponder. I think you will get up with a 5."

Alfie put his hand under the 5 iron and lifted it slightly. Tom pushed the 5 iron down and took the 4 iron out. He poised and hit the ball right over the back, at which point, Alf recalled, he was annoyed because Tom hadn't listened to him. Uncharacteristically he walked off, leaving Tom on his own. Tom put a spring into his step and catching Alfie up said, "What are we going to do now, Alf?"

His reply was, "Unless you've got a pointing trowel in your bag, we're screwed."

Tom addressed the ball, played it against the wall and bounced it back onto the green. They didn't win the match, but came second.

Alfie's dad, Ted, continued to work at Royal Birkdale and friend John remembers seeing eighty-one-year-old Ted riding his bike home from work one summer evening at the end of the 70s. Ted used to ride exceptionally slowly and it was a mystery that he stayed upright.

John opened the door of The Crown public house and Alfie looked up.

"How are you doing, my old pal?"

"Not bad, thanks, Alf. I've just seen your dad outside, riding home."

"Cheers, John, I'll ask him in for a pint."

Alfie jumped up and went to the door. Ted was pedalling slowly from Arundel Road, across the busy Liverpool Road without stopping at the junction or even looking either way to see if anything was coming towards him. Cars flew past him, swerving to avoid knocking him off.

"Dad! Dad! What the hell are you doing? You're going to get yourself bloody well killed, man. You're supposed to stop, there's a Stop sign there."

"Not for pensioners, Alfie. Not for pensioners," Ted called back. "And anyway, if I stop, I can't get started again."

Alfie was a hard-working, hard-playing grafter who earned and lost a fortune in his time. He liked a flutter on the horses but it had to be a grey. If it wasn't a grey horse, he just didn't bother. Son Johnny said he saw his dad lose £9,000 on a bet once - just like that. He bet on a horse and lost the whole lot. He didn't even flinch, and considering it was at a time when you could buy a house for £10,000, it was a significant amount of money. At the time, son John and his wife were looking to buy a house which was on the market for just under £10,000 and John said he felt sick at the thought of his dad losing as much money as the house cost, but Alf just accepted it as a part of his life. Pat on the other hand, when she found out, flew off the handle and berated him for losing so much in one go. Both Pat and Alfie would agree that his gambling was one of the main reasons they argued so often.

Alf's life was a roller coaster of exceptional highs and debilitating lows and he played as hard as he worked. In a good week, he could earn many thousands of pounds. The betting occasionally paid off as well.

Son John was 23 years old when he reluctantly took a bet in to his local bookmakers for his dad. He told him he thought he had gone mad as he wanted to place £100 on an around-the-clock accumulator which was 13 bets; if one bet wins, the money is automatically used as a stake for the next race. It cost £1,300 to place the bet and John had the money in an envelope inside his jacket pocket. He ran up Portland Street and into the local bookmakers, who knew John and would take any bet from him.

The first two races came in at 20-1 and 4-1 which meant there was an amazing amount of money going onto the next race. Unfortunately, the last horse didn't win, but Alf had a combination of odds and bets attached to it and it was a complicated set up. Alf asked John to go with him to pick up his winnings on the Monday morning and just before they entered the bookies, Alf said to John, "Now then, you were calling me an idiot, weren't you?"

"Well, yes, but the bet never came up, did it? You've won nothing."

"Just watch this, son. Just watch this."

John stared aghast as Alf walked up to the counter, gave the bookie his chit and in return the teller handed him just under £21,000 in winnings.

Alf and Pat followed many superstitions. On the first practice day of a major tournament, when caddying for Tom, Alf phoned son Mick and said, "We're going to win this match, Mick. Get hold of as much money as you can and put it on us." And the reason for Alf's confidence? When he had taken the cover off Tom's driver that morning there had been a swarm of money spiders inside it which Alf took as a good omen. The family put on what they could and sure enough, Tom went on to win the competition.

On another occasion, Alfie's gut feelings paid off again when the favourite to win the match told him he wasn't feeling 100% and just hoped he could manage to finish the course. Again, Alf was convinced that his own man would go on to win, prompting him to phone Mick to persuade him to put a bet on his player. Alfie's tips didn't always come off, but once more his man went on to win convincingly and family and friends won out to the bookmakers.

When Alf was caddy master at Walton Heath he caddied each week for a well-established and wealthy horse owner who trained and rode his horses at Epsom, only a few miles away from the club.

When he and his golfing partner played their weekend game, they had a £40 bet on who would win that week. One week he promised Alf a tip if he won that Saturday which, in due course, he did. He gave Alf his wages and asked if he would like his tip in money or a tip on a horse. There was of course no competition, and Alf asked for the name of the horse so he could have a flutter. The man told him the name and said that if Alfie bet on it and the horse didn't win, he would give him the money back out of his own pocket. Again, Alf phoned the family and said to place large bets if they could.

Mick won over £700. Pat and John put on £180 - all their

savings - and the horse romped in at 10-1.

Alf used to tell the tale of the day he put £200 on a horse with a well-known bookmaker. The race was due to start at 2.00 and Alfie hurried into the shop as it came up to the race time. It came in at 20-1 but, although they had taken the bet, it had been 2 seconds past 2 so they refused to pay out, giving him back his stake money only.

Alf was incensed. He argued they had taken the bet so they should pay out, but the company refused, saying that was the rule so they weren't going to pay. Alf went to the local newspaper and told them what had happened. They ran a story, and although the company still wouldn't pay, it would not have done their reputation any good, especially when, the following week, the paper printed another story with Alf holding up the banner for a rival company, showing him putting on a bet for that year's Open.

Between 1979 and 1986 professional golfer-turned-television presenter Peter Alliss hosted seven series of *Around with Alliss*, in which he played a few holes of golf and chatted with a variety of famous people on different courses around the UK. When he was due to interview Tom Watson, they agreed that the programme would be recorded just prior to one of the big championships and Alfie was, once more, caddying for Tom. At that time caddies were not usually accepted in the hotels the players stayed in, but because of the programme, the BBC put Alf up in a five-star hotel and he was happy to stay there while they filmed. Alf was going through a bad patch at that time and he arrived at the hotel with just £3.50 in his pocket.

Alfie knew he would be paid a substantial sum for caddying and he didn't need much money because the TV company were paying his expenses, but he intended going up to his room until he met up with Tom the following morning, when he could get some cash off him if necessary.

As per his usual arrangements, Alfie took with him the plastic carrier bag that was his luggage. He put it down while he checked in and a bell boy approached him, picking up the bag to carry it for him.

"No, that's Ok," Alf protested, but the boy insisted.

"That's Ok, sir. It is our pleasure to serve you." And he duly walked towards the lift to show Alfie to his room.

"Where would you like your luggage, sir?" he asked a bemused Alfie as he swung open the door, allowing Alf to walk into the room before him.

"Oh, erm, anywhere - the chair will do."

"Thank you, sir." And he carefully placed the supermarket bag down on the chair as though it was diamond encrusted. Before leaving, he held his hand out waiting for a tip, giving a subtle cough for recognition. Alfie's heart sank as he retrieved the £3.50 from his trouser pocket and deposited it in the bellboy's hand. The boy gave him a disgruntled, disgusted half-grimace and majestically swept out of the room as he thanked Alf for the gratuity.

Later that evening, Alf went down to the lounge area and sat, people-watching, considering the times in his early career when he had slept in the car, in bushes, open shelters, anywhere dry that he could get some sleep for the night. He would regale his friends with, 'The amount of times I've slept with Mrs. Greenleaves is no body's business …'

Alf was continuing to daydream when an American gentleman, who was there to watch the golf, asked if the seat opposite Alf was free, and they got talking about the ensuing competition. The gentleman asked Alfie if he was playing the next day, or there to watch.

"No, I'm here to caddy."

"Oh, right. Who are you caddying for?"

"Tom Watson."

"Tom Watson? You're kidding, right? Hey guys, this man is caddying for Tom Watson tomorrow. How about that?" And before long, Alf was surrounded by a group of Americans, all of whom wanted to buy him a drink. Que Sera, Sera.

8

The 80s

In 1980 Tom Watson won the Open at Muirfield with Alfie, who was still caddy master at Walton Heath at this point. Greg Norman won the Suntory Match Play at Wentworth with Bobby Leigh, and Teddy Halsall caddied for Johnnie Miller when Miller made a comeback in the Lancome event in Paris. Miller invited Teddy and his wife to America for a holiday in gratitude, a trip they thoroughly enjoyed.

Alf earned a decent amount for the 1982 Open with Tom Watson, but on his return, he would go to the pub and the crowd around him would be hanging onto his every word and enjoying his generosity until the money dried up. He bought drinks for everyone, and if someone said they liked a particular item of Alfie's he would say, 'Take it, have it - I don't need it'. And he would press the item onto the individual even if they didn't really want it. In Alf's ethos, the fact that they admired it meant they should have it.

Alf always looked smart, even in those times when fortune didn't shine on him. Unlike some of the caddies, who would look unkempt or dishevelled, Alf would be bathed, shoes shined, trousers pressed, with a good haircut and either a roll neck sweater or one of the cashmere jumpers he was famous for owning. And of course, invariably, one of his numerous 'bonnets' to set off his outfit.

In those days, the likes of Tom Watson would be sponsored by either Ram or Scott & Lyle, and many of the caddies would go into the Pro shop at Royal Birkdale and ask for a top to wear to look smart when they caddied. The shop and/or clothing manufacturer would be delighted to allow the likes of Alfie to wear one of the jumpers because they knew there was a likelihood it would be seen on TV or in the national media and would therefore be an excellent source of advertising for them.

As said previously, on more than one occasion someone had admired Alf's top. 'Hey, Alf, I like your sweater'. No more was said, but Alf would strip it off and give it to the individual. He gave more jumpers away than he could remember and never tired of giving generous gifts to his friends and family.

On one occasion however he lost more jumpers in an instant than he could have imagined when he took his clothes to the local laundrette.

"Service wash, please, Mary."

"No problem, Alfie. Leave it till about ten o'clock tomorrow -

I've got a few on today. How did the competition go last week?"

"Not bad, Mary, not bad. Didn't win, but we came close. Next time, eh?"

Alf went back to his flat and looked at the racing page to see which greys were running. That evening, despite having earned so much at the Open, Alf was sitting in the Mason's nursing a pint. One of his mates asked why he was only having the one. Alf said he was broke. "I gave it all to sick animals, mate."

"Really, Alf? That's good of you."

"Yes, Fred, but I didn't know they were sick when I backed them."

The next day Alf went back to the laundrette for his washing. The assistant sheepishly handed over his bags of laundry.

"Er, I did your washing and dried it all off, Alf. But I think I should warn you there was a slight problem."

Alf started taking his clothes out of the bag.

"Ok, Mary, don't worry, I'm sure nothing is so bad we need to worry about it, my dear."

One by one, he took out his precious cashmeres, all lovingly washed then dried by Mary. Now anyone who has ever tumble-dried a woollen jumper will have spotted the inevitable here. Each one had been shrunk to a quarter of its size by the heat of the dryer. Alf held up the first one to his chest. It might have fitted an eight-year-old but would never fit Alf again.

"A *slight* flaming problem?" he exploded. "Good God, woman, if I wanted to dress the gnomes in the garden I'd see a dressmaker."

Many of the caddies were given promotional items or kept small items of memorabilia such as tees and golf balls that had been used by famous golfers. When they got short of money they would often sell the items to make a few pounds, and there is many a fan who now owns a ball that genuinely used to belong to one of the famous. However, there was an unscrupulous element who knew exactly how to work the system.

"Oh, my God, you should have seen Sam Snead hit that ball. The crowd went wild. Next shot, it went in the rough and he couldn't find it. He had to drop a ball. Afterwards I went in and waded around a bit. Found it in ten minutes. If you look closely you can see his mark. Of course, it's not as clear as it used to be. I've carried that ball around with me for years and it breaks my heart to let it go, but I'm down on my uppers right now and I don't know how I can pay my rent this week, so if you really want it and promise to look after it, it's yours for a tenner."

The next week they would have a similar ball on sale to another punter in a different pub. It didn't matter who the golfer was, the tournament and course changed accordingly, but the story and the golf ball was good for a few pints, time and time again.

Alf caddied for Tom Watson when he won his fourth Open in July 1982 at Troon.

American Bobby Clampett dominated days one and two and remained top on the leader board on day three. However, he had dropped to joint 10th by the end of the match, which was subsequently won by Tom and Alfie. In 1983 Bobby caddied for Greg Norman when he won his second Suntory World Match Play at Wentworth. Greg defeated Nick Faldo 3 & 2 in the final and claimed victory on the 34th.

In the same year, Alfie caddied for Tom again when he won his fifth and second consecutive Open, which was played at Royal Birkdale. It was also Tom's eighth and final major championship win of his career although he has continued to play in many major competitions since.

Alfie would go on to say about the 1983 Open: 'In round one we were 4 under and joint second with Lee Trevino. On day two we were 7 under with Stadler leading. On day three Tom took a penalty drop early on'. He said that probably the most memorable shot of the match was when Bill Rodgers got an albatross on the par 5.

Alf went into the Masons after the competition and Judy, the landlady, congratulated Alf on his and Tom's success.

"That's six big ones now, isn't it, Alf?"

"Oh no, love, it's seven. I won the Open with Reg Brown in 1936. That was at Birkdale as well."

Alfie continued to caddy for Tom for another two years but Tom didn't win anything significant in this time. Alf was paid a decent wage on the day and given a sizeable tip by Tom for supporting him. Consequently, Alf decided to get onto the property ladder so as to put some security behind him. He bought a house in the prestigious Weld Road; this cost him £11,000.

These days it would be worth many hundreds of thousands of pounds. However, six months later, Alf, having spent up again, sold the house on for just £8,000.

There is no doubt that Alf could have been a very rich man if he had handled his money more carefully and invested wisely. Alf himself said that in one year, when Tom had won the Open amongst other competitions, he, Alfie, had earned just over £70,000. But, as previously stated, he had a big heart and couldn't resist a sob story. If someone was down on their luck, Alfie was more than happy to help them out. However, he dreaded the thought of being in debt and his bills were all paid up front. In fact, his gas and electric were always in credit and he ensured everything was paid out before spending on himself. What is sad is that, although his funeral was paid for, when he died he had just a few hundred pounds to his name.

Alf adored his family, and although his didn't always show it he had a great depth of pride and love for them. Although he and Pat had periodically lived apart, he would do anything for her, and if she needed him he was there.

In 1985, when Alf's niece, Debbie, was due to marry friend and surrogate son John, she asked him to give her away as she had no contact with her biological father. Alf had been just like a father to her since she was born - she was the daughter he had never had. He instantly agreed, and at the speech Alf thanked everyone, regaled them with the obligatory funny stories, then said:

"In all my time, I have made some outstanding accomplishments, but when Debbie asked me to give her away I consider this to be the biggest accomplishment of my life."

Alf's eyes misted over and he looked at Debbie, who was dabbing at her eyes. There were many handkerchiefs out and noses being blown. Deb and Alf smiled at each other fondly before he went on to finish his speech.

John and Deb had numerous female guests at the wedding and Alfie put on a show, fussing over each one alike. As he was introduced to them, he took their hand and kissed it, smiling a beaming smile that lit up his twinkling eyes and made every lady feel she was the only woman in the room. John's aunts would talk about Alfie on many future occasions as they were truly smitten with him.

Unlike Alfie and Albert, who never played a day's golf, Teddy and Bobby were both good golfers. As previously said, Ted and Albert were real friends and usually caddied together. They were a lot younger than Alf and saw it as a quest to be as successful as he was. They had seen Alf and Bobby's successes, Bobby being probably the first of the four to win anything in the way of a big prize, but the potential was there for them all to win big and there was always a rivalry between them as to who could be the best.

Bobby, even though he was caddying for many famous golfers, could never resist the urge to take on a golfing challenge himself. Amongst other professionals, the two Tomlinson brothers from the Park Golf Club had come up against him on occasion. He would say to whichever pro was on duty, 'Well, you hit the ball a long way today, son, but I bet you £10 I can beat you'. Not only could he beat them by hitting the ball further, but he could drink an inordinate amount of beer and then do it just as well!

Sometimes he would also challenge the professional to a game and purposely lose to him. He would then settle in the club house and drink 18 or 19 pints of beer, then raise the wager again. At this point he would invariably say, in a feigned drunken slur, 'Do you know, even though I've had a drink, I think I can still beat you'.

"You didn't beat me today."

"Well, even though I've had a drink, I still think I could beat you now."

Eagerly, the pro would think he could increase his £10 win to £30 or so, and they would go out to the first tee followed by a group of thirty or forty people who had been watching the discussion in the club. He would tee the ball up and give it the most enormous whack, leaving the hapless professional scratching his head thinking, 'What happened there?'

He repeated this routine on more than one occasion.

Once, he played off a two handicap; the best part of his game was driving the ball. He was a big powerful man but he also had the finesse and timing needed to be a more than competent opponent.

Bobby Leigh was a character but he wasn't like most of the other lads, who were rough and ready and streetwise. He was up to the challenge of travelling but was more refined and gentlemanly. On one occasion in the mid-80s, Bobby had arranged to go on holiday with a lady companion. However, he didn't want the others to know he was going away with her because he knew they would make fun of him, so he told them he was caddying in Hawaii for Greg Norman.

At the end of the week there were four or five caddies sitting chatting in the pub following a local competition, when one of them said:

"I saw one of your mates yesterday."

"Who was that, then?"

"Bobby Leigh."

"Where was that, then? He's on holiday."

"He was in Scarborough."

The man had been on holiday for the week with his family and on the last day had seen Bobby and his girlfriend walking down the promenade hand in hand. Two days later Bobby returned home not realising he had been spotted.

"So how did Hawaii go then, Bobby?"

"It was a good trip, thanks."

"Did Greg win then?"

"No, but he played well."

The caddy smirked. "Good, good. So how did you do on the promenade at Scarborough, then?"

"What do you mean? Don't be so daft. What are you going on about?"

"Hawaii Five-0 - you've been on holiday in Scarborough, not caddying."

"Well, I couldn't tell you lot, could I!"

As the caddy grinned at Bobby, someone started humming the

theme tune to 'Hawaii Five-0', which was a popular TV programme=that year, and from then on he earned himself the nickname McGarrett, which was the leading character's name.

By now Alfie had caddied in many pro-am matches and had worked with some extremely famous golfers. Once more he was caddying in a pro-am at Gleneagles with Tom O'Connor. When Tom called to pick up Alfie at 8.30 the next morning, Alfie was carrying his belongings in two KwikSave carrier bags.

"All right, Alf? Is that it? Where are you staying tonight?"

Alf held up the carrier bags with a flourish. "Anywhere they take matching suitcases, Tom, anywhere they take matching suitcases."

The Ladies British Open was held at Royal Birkdale in 1986. British-born Laura Jane Davies, now Dame, prevailed against her American opposition, Peggy Conley and Debbie Massey, while holding off the challenge from Marta Figueras-Dotti, winning by four shots. Laura Jane Davies has been called the most accomplished English female golfer of all times, and once more, the Birkdale Boys went forward to caddy at the tournament.

In the late '80s a couple of Alf's friends were going to play golf at a small golf course in the Midlands, and Alfie went with them to caddy. They were booked in for the day and wanted to start early so they could get back for dinner. John phoned and asked the professional if it was Ok to go down early and he said there was no problem with this, but there wouldn't be anyone there early in the morning. He gave directions, explaining that as they went past the ninth, they could call in at the professionals' shop and pay the green fees, then continue to the 10th.

They played the front first nine and called in as planned. As John entered, Alfie stopped by the door, waiting to carry on. The assistant pro started nudging the professional and indicating that Alfie was standing by the door. The professional pushed the assistant out of the way and made a beeline for John, saying,

"I am sorry, sir, but I don't recognise you."

To which John replied, "There's no reason you would. You don't know me, but I rang last night to ask if it was Ok to go out first thing this morning."

The pro replied, "Forgive me if I'm wrong - that *is* Alfie Fyles caddying for you, isn't it?"

"Yes, it is Alfie Fyles but ..."

"Well, pardon me, but I thought you might be a professional or a man of importance."

"No, he's my mate."

"Well, would you mind if I ask Alf a question?"

"Not at all - Alf, he wants you."

"Our chairman, Mr X, is a very, very good golfer and apparently, you caddied for him many years ago."

It transpired that the chairman's claim to fame was that Alfie had caddied for him and he told everyone that Tom Watson's caddy was his caddy before he became Tom Watson's.

Alfie gasped. "No, not really, not Mr X! Get out of it. Do you know what, John? I caddied for him when he was a boy."

The pro asked Alfie if he would mind if he rang the chairman to tell him he was in the shop, and he made the phone call there and then.

Alf said, "Tell Mr X I will call in when we have finished our round."

The pro replied, "He's on his way over now, as we speak."

John told Alfie they would finish their round by themselves and Alfie should go into the club house to greet the chairman; they would see him in the bar afterwards.

This was agreed and they finished their round, put the clubs away and entered the club house, where a group of about thirty people were huddled around a table on which there were numerous empty whiskey glasses (because everyone who joined the conversation bought Alfie a drink). He was playing the showman, making stories up as he went along, the chairman interspersing Alfie's stories with the tales he had been telling people for years.

"Your chairman is possibly one of the finest amateur golfers I have ever caddied for. What did you get on the 17th - was it a three? I'm sure it was a three and you *whipped* them, didn't you? Didn't you *whip* them?"

The chairman was saying in a low voice, "Yes, three on the 17th, three, yes."

The tales went on and the more exuberant Alfie got, the more drinks arrived. When it was time to leave, Alfie waved a cheery goodbye saying, "I'll see you again, sir."

As they left the club house John asked if the man was really that good.

"I don't know, John, but he's a bloody good liar. I've never met him in my life before, the lying b*****d."

"So, he was telling porkies, Alf? Why didn't you say something?"

"Hey, John, there's a lot of whiskies go with porkies."

That evening the trio went out for dinner to a little pub and they were relaxing, recalling golfing tales, joking and recalling the story of the chairman from earlier in the day. They were enjoying the ambiance and around 10.30pm a lady came over and said, "I don't know you three gentlemen from Adam, but I've been watching you all evening and you haven't stopped laughing all night. Right through, you've been talking and laughing. It's heart-warming. I wish my Stan could have been here to see you," and off she went to sit back down in her seat.

About half an hour later, she got up and came across to them again.

"I'm off now, boys," she said. "It's been lovely to see you this evening."

At this Alf asked for her hand. The lady proffered it and he said, "Only - I read fortunes and I just want to see what the future holds for you." Intrigued, she leaned in closer, waiting eagerly for what he was going to say next.

"You've got a new man."

"Oh no, I haven't!" she declared.

"You don't realise it yet, but you've got a new man - and what is this I can see?" Following her lifeline, he continued, "You are being influenced by someone whose name begins with an S. Does that mean anything to you?"

"Could it be an older man?" she enquired, forgetting the earlier conversation. Then she gasped. "My Stan. I'll bet it's my Stan."

"It *is* your Stan. He is saying he's gone and you should enjoy yourself. Have a nice time."

She filled up and continued, "It's my Stan and I've come out to celebrate his birthday. How do you know all this?"

"I'm telling you, I can read the future."

"But you said I've got a *new* man."

Alfie lowered his voice. "You have, you have, and Stan is saying go out and have a nice time, don't hold back. If you find somebody attractive and if you find, soon, that same person holding your hand, don't hold back."

"You bugger!" she snapped and she pulled her hand away, just as Alfie said, "What size was Stan? Are there any suits in the wardrobe?"

"You bugger." But she left the pub giggling and smiling.

9

Beginning of the End

Around the same time that Alfie caddied for Tom in his last Open win, he rented the flat in Birkdale village previously referred to, the one that backed on to the dairy farm where he had worked as a teenager. He was fiercely independent and, when the times were good, enjoyed a good life, keeping the flat clean and doing all his own cooking. On Sundays he would make a pan of stew, or scouse as it is known in and around Merseyside, and he would often invite the family to come and enjoy it with him. However, when he was down on his uppers he often scraped around for a decent meal, and the fair-weather friends that had surrounded him and helped him spend his wages were nowhere to be seen.

One day at the end of the 80s, son John went into the Masons to see Alf and have a pint with him. Someone said, "Your dad's not very well, John. He keeps slurring his words and he doesn't recognise me."

"Hi, Dad. How's it going?"

Alfie mumbled incoherently.

"What, mate? What did you say? Who am I, Dad?"

"What'cha mean? Bloody stupid. You're John." It was followed by a string of burbled words.

"Well, why are you speaking funny, Dad?"

John could see Alfie needed medical help and luckily there was a phone box just outside the pub, from which he called for an ambulance. When the paramedics arrived, they asked Alf to smile, but he couldn't.

The ambulance man turned to John and said, "I think he's had a seizure."

"What's that, mate? Sorry, I don't understand."

The paramedic explained that it looked as though Alf had had a stroke and that time was of the essence. They needed to get him to hospital immediately if they were to save his life or get him back some quality of life. They got on either side of him and tried to stand him up. Alf got a grip on his pint glass with his good hand and protested vehemently because they were trying to move him.

"Gnnnn. Bgrr fff. Gnnnnn." And he set all his weight down as he held on to his drink with a vicelike grip.

"Come on now, Mr. Fyles, we need to go," one of the men pleaded, recognising the urgency of getting him to hospital. But Alf cursed and swore incoherently and refused point blank to go until he had finished the drink he had paid for.

Alf had indeed had a mild stroke and although his progress was slow, he made a full recovery. However, the GP advised him to move out of his first-floor flat and find one on the ground floor. He acquired sheltered accommodation in the Marshside area of the town, and friends John and Billy helped him move, John using his Range Rover as it was cheaper than hiring a removal van, and because Alf really didn't have enough possessions to warrant hiring one.

As they moved backwards and forwards with his belongings, among them was an antique canvas golf bag and wooden clubs. Alf didn't rate collecting possessions, but this set meant a lot to him and he had kept it close to his heart for many years since he acquired it as a thank-you from a grateful punter early in his career. John and Bill carried the heavier items and Alf took what he could to the car.

As he picked up the canvas bag to put it in the boot, he tripped, and the clubs cascaded one by one onto the road.

"Some kind of freaking caddy *you* are, Alfie Fyles." And the three of them fell about laughing.

For all the money he had amassed and lost, for all the interviews and the notoriety, Alfie was a man's man and had no frills, airs or graces.

Bobby Leigh, now blind and having grown both in status and stature, would sit in the corner at the Park Golf club and recognise everyone by their voice.

John walked in the door one evening and said, "You all right, Bob?"

"Aye, not so bad, Fyles's lad."

They had a couple of drinks and Bobby decided it was time to go. He walked out of the door and straight into the path of a youth riding a Raleigh moped. Bang. It hit him full on and the rider went flying off into the road. Bobby didn't flinch, though, and said, "Bloody hell, lad, I'm big enough, didn't you see me?"

"I did, mate, yes, but I didn't have enough petrol to go around you."

Pat continued to suffer with heart problems and sadly passed away in 1990 from heart failure. Alfie was devastated and grieved heavily for her. His grief was to be impacted further when in December 1990 he got a phone call.

"Alfie?" His sister sounded desperate.

"Hi, love, what's the problem?"

"Dad's ill."

"What do you mean by ill?"

It had only been a few weeks since Alfie had seen him and he had been his usual self with no signs of ill health. Ted Fyles had retired from Royal Birkdale in 1987 aged nearly ninety. He continued to ride his bike everywhere and tend his garden. The family visited often and he enjoyed his retirement.

"We think he had a stroke a few hours ago. He's in the hospital and Mam asked me to ring you. He might not last the night."

"I'm on my way."

Alf got to the hospital as fast as he could, running inside to reception. They directed him to the ward and Margaret sat outside looking frail and worried. The rest of the family, sons, daughters, grandchildren, great grandchildren, filled the corridor and waiting room. Albert stood by Margaret's side with his hand on her shoulder. Alf ignored him as he went over and crouched down beside her.

"You Ok, Mam? What's happening?"

"They're doing tests."

Margaret didn't want to talk. If she talked about Ted's condition it would make it real. She wanted to go back to yesterday when her Teddy was laughing and joking with her. She thought about what had happened that morning.

Ted had not wanted to get up and dressed. That wasn't unusual. At their age neither of them had needed to get up so early any more. Since his retirement, he had become listless and uncoordinated. His sense of humour was still evident but he had lost his verve. Like so many people, retirement served to incapacitate him.

Margaret had left him to sleep, taking him a cup of tea mid-morning. Ted had made a gurgling sound in the back of his throat and looked helplessly at her, pleading silently for her to help him.

She had gone next door to where her grandson lived.

"Quickly! Quickly! Your granddad is ill"

He phoned for an ambulance and they waited at Ted's side, Margaret holding his hand and talking quietly, up against his face. Margaret thought about her reaction as she had said to him,

"Teddy Fyles, I need you to stay with me. Don't leave me, Ted. Please don't leave me. Everything will be OK. I promise." On and on she went, soothingly, lovingly, until the emergency services arrived and they manoeuvred him into the back of the ambulance. In the hospital corridor Alfie hugged his mother. They didn't need to say anything. He held her and she pushed her face into his shoulder.

"Oh Alf, what will I do if ..." She couldn't carry on.

They waited for what seemed like an eternity until the doctor took them into a side room. Teddy's children went in, the rest of the family remaining in the corridor.

He confirmed that Teddy had indeed had a stroke. He explained that many people have strokes and recover. One in five people will have a stroke and not even know it. However, Teddy's age was a barrier to full recovery.

Alf knew the doctor was talking but he couldn't take in what was being said.

Soon it was acknowledged that Ted was almost certainly not going to recover. His vital signs were weakening and the doctor prepared the family to accept his death.

"If there is anyone you think will want to see Ted, I suggest you call them to come soon."

For days, there was a constant stream of people going in and out of the ward. Including Teddy Halsall and Bobby Leigh.

When someone is close to death the carers or nurses try to put them on 'the vigil'. This means they are never left unattended and are cared for constantly, so they don't die alone.

Unfortunately there isn't always the staff to do this, and in Ted's case it was superfluous as he had family and/or friends with him around the clock. Margaret insisted on staying by his side, sleeping fitfully in the chair. When they occasionally persuaded her to go home and get a bath or get changed, she was back within hours, unable to rest knowing he was in a stark, clinical hospital room.

A few days later, Alf arrived around nine o'clock at night. He told his siblings he would stay the night so they could go home and get some rest.

In the early hours of December 9th, Ted opened his eyes and looked towards the topmost corner of the room. He cried out, "Ok, Ok. Don't shout. I'm coming, Mam."

Margaret jumped and slowly pulled her gaze from his face, reluctantly glancing over her shoulder to look at what he was seeing. Alf too was looking intently, but there was nothing there.

Ted picked fitfully at his sheets and was agitated. He was distressed. Margaret took his hand and slowly he calmed down and closed his eyes again.

"It's Ok, Teddy, I'm here," she crooned to him.

His perspiration increased and his colour decreased. His lips becoming bluish tinged and his breathing laboured.

"Oh my God, Alf, he's on his way out."

"No, Mam, I'm sure it's a blip. Just you wait, he'll come around and be as good as new tomorrow." He didn't believe it of course, but he wanted to reassure his mother and didn't know what else to say.

At eight the next morning Teddy opened his eyes and smiled at Margaret. His breath was short and he had developed a blotchy pallor, but he was fully conscious. "Still got them eyes in the back of your head, Margie?"

"Always will have, Teddy Fyles, and I will still watch you when my back is turned."

"Then go and watch me as you bring me a cup of tea, woman."

Margaret didn't know what to think. It had been weeks since he had eaten or drunk anything significant. It was such a welcome surprise that he was coherent that she didn't think about the incongruence of his request.

"Ok, my love, if that's what you want."

"I'll go, Mam," Alf said. "I can't expect you to walk to the nurses' station."

"Don't interfere, son. Your mother has been bringing me a cup of tea in bed for breakfast since I retired. Let her go."

Margaret smiled indulgently. She stood awkwardly, arthritic joints creaking as she groaned, "Oh my word, Teddy, I'm getting too old for all of this."

She left the room and slowly made her way along the corridor. Teddy looked at Alf pleadingly. "Look after her, son." He nodded towards the door and looked upwards. He closed his eyes. "I'm coming, Mam. I'm coming."

He breathed noisily, his breath now a rattle. He took on a waxy yellowish pallor as he said again, "Look after her, Alfie."

Confused, Alf didn't know what he should do. Should he ring for the nurse? Wait until Margaret got back? Go and fetch her to come back to Ted? After what seemed like an eternity but was probably less than a minute, he pressed the nurse call, tears streaming down his face as reality hit him.

The nurse arrived before Margaret got back and she ushered Alfie out of the room.

"Just give me a minute, Mr Fyles. Go and sit with your mother until I see what's going on."

He met Margaret a few yards down the corridor.

"Mam …"

"I know, son, he didn't want me to see him go. He *has* gone, hasn't he?"

"I don't know, Mam, but I think so. The nurse is just with him." Margaret sat wearily down on the bench seat and crumpled. She cried silently at first then broke into great heavy sobs which shook her body, as the irrevocability of the death of her soulmate hit her. She was still crying as Ted's family and friends began to visit, each one to be told he had finally succumbed to the only certainty in life.

The funeral was arranged for the following week, leaving from their home in Suffolk Road. The house was wall-to-wall relatives, and many friends and acquaintances gathered at the church for the ceremony, including many workers and members of the Royal Birkdale, plus Ted's friends David and Thomas, now pensioners themselves, walking side by side into the church. What was noticeable though was the presence of Alfie, Albert, Teddy Halsall and Bobby Leigh. This was the first time the four had been together for many years, and although Alf and Albert were still not on talking terms, nonetheless, standing on opposite sides of the grave, they were all together for the day.

In 1993, Alf had a heart attack, followed by another stroke which once more put him into hospital, and while carrying out further tests, the medics found something that was far more ominous. With a great deal of trepidation son John agreed to accompany Alf to the consultant to get the results. At this point he was still getting confused and calling people by the wrong name, and as they sat together in the consultant's office he dropped the bombshell.

"Mr Fyles, I will come straight to the point. I'm afraid we have found a shadow on your lung and nine times out of ten this is caused by cancer."

Turning to John, Alf said, "Have you heard this joker, Johnnie? Are you having a bloody laugh?"

"I'm afraid not, Mr. Fyles, it is very serious and we need to ..."

"Ah, behave yourself. He's f****d, John. Come on, son. Come on, *come on*."

And with that he jumped up and turned towards the door at a pace. John apologised to the consultant for his father's outburst and, turning to his father, continued, "Just a minute, Dad. You need to take this seriously. Listen to what the man has to say."

"For Christ's sake, John, I've not got cancer. He doesn't know what the hell he's talking about."

"But Mr Fyles, you really need to keep this appointment. You may need treatment and Clatterbridge is the leading cancer hospital in the north west."

Reluctantly, Alfie agreed, and within days John and Alf saw a specialist where it was confirmed that he did indeed have a tumour in his lung. He was admitted to Clatterbridge and went on to have radiotherapy

Son John and his wife Jackie went to visit Alfie while he was in the hospital, but he wasn't by his bed. They went searching for him and found him sitting smoking outside, still hooked up to the treatment.

"Come on, lad, we'll go for a smoke." Alfie gestured towards the main building.

"What? You can't go for a ciggie in a hospital."

"Give over, man, of course we can. Follow me to the smoking room."

They duly followed, and as Alf opened the door to the rest-room they were met with a thick blanket of smoke; half a dozen patients at different stages of treatment sat puffing away. All the windows were open but it was having little effect on the veil of smoke that hung in the air.

When Alf returned home from hospital, the family visited him as often as possible. Different relatives would take him a meal which he just had to warm up, or a small bottle of whiskey, his favourite tipple, but invariably it would still be there, untouched, the following day as he could no longer eat or drink.

They saw a deterioration in him as the weeks progressed, which was heart-breaking. Son John went to visit Alfie every lunch time, and on one visit Alf told him that he didn't feel as bad that day, so John asked if he would like to go for a pint, but he refused. John realised at this point how serious it was - up until then there always seemed to be some hope of recovery.

Alf was a proud, strong, independent man and hated the fact that people had to do anything for him, but with the cancer and the treatment he had started to lose control of his bodily functions. One lunch time when John visited, Alf sat crying as he had had an accident. It was the first-time John had ever seen his dad cry, and it was like a sledge hammer blow as he realised that Alf really was losing his battle with the cancer.

By now he couldn't get out to the bookies to put a bet on and had largely lost all interest anyway. One day he told John and Jackie he would have liked a flutter, but he couldn't be bothered.

"Here, give me the paper, Alf, I'll pick you a winner," Jackie said. She picked two greys and placed the bet for him. They both came in at a decent price and when Jackie took his winnings he said, "Bleeding marvellous. It's the first time in my life I've had a double up and I'm ruddy well dying. I can't even spend it."

Alfie was in the local hospice and had many visitors before he passed away including close friend John Murray, who asked Alf if he had any regrets about his life.

"Oh God, yes, John, many regrets, but I guess splitting up with Pat rates as one of the biggest. Mind you, the one that cuts me up the most is that I never got to finish my book. I would have loved to tell the world my story and now, it just won't happen." As an afterthought, he added, "Oh, and I wish the Inland Revenue hadn't read the damned article about Gay Brewer dropping me the £1,000 tip in 1967. They hounded me for years over it."

The rift between Alfie and brother Albert never healed, and while in the hospice, Albert and wife Pamela tried to visit him. Niece Debbie saw them arrive, but when the nurse came into his room to tell him they were there, he politely told her to send them away.

"But Alfie, he's your brother and he's come to see you."

"I SAID SEND HIM AWAY," Alf shouted, and became distressed. "For God's sake, Debbie, send him away. I don't want to see him. Please, please Deb, tell him to go."

10

Saying Goodbye

As Alf's sons John and Mick were sitting with Alf a few hours before his death, he said to them, "I just want to let you know that I've had a brilliant life and enjoyed everything I've done. I've got only one regret, which I've told you both before. That is, I wish I could have changed how it turned out with your mum. But whatever you do, don't worry about me because I'm just going to see her now."

Alf deteriorated over the next few hours and passed away on 7th March, 1994, in Queenscourt Hospice, Southport, with niece Debbie at one side of him and daughter-in-law Jackie at the other.

The family were given ten days to clear Alf's council-owned flat in Fleetwood Road, but it was heart-breaking how little he had to be disposed of. He died with just £300 to his name and had only a few changes of clothing despite having built up an extensive wardrobe over the years. Basically, he had given away most of his clothes and belongings and those that were left were only fit to be skipped. Alf had lived a life of major ups and downs and the only thing he owned that was of any value was a television he had bought a few months previously. As son John carried it out of the tiny flat, Alf's next-door-neighbour approached him.

"Excuse me, excuse me, I'm sorry to hear about Alfie."

"Thanks for that, love, but it was to be expected. We were with him in his last few hours."

"Oh bless. Look, I might be out of order here, but he had just bought a new television licence and …"

Confused, and thinking she was asking for it, John said if he came across it, he would drop it in for her.

"Oh no, I didn't mean that, but you can get a refund on it if you contact the TV people."

John thanked her for her concern and it was disconcerting that they found evidence that Alf had been ill for many months before going into hospital. It looked as though he had tried to hide the full extent of his illness from the family - that was the type of man Alfie was, generous to a fault - usually at his own expense.

Many people attended Alfie's funeral to pay their last respects, including Albert, although he stayed away from the main body of mourners.

In 2004, when Bobby Leigh died of diabetes, Peter Thomson wrote the following testimonial:

Melbourne, Mar 4th 2004

'Jack (Bobby) Leigh was my friend as well as my caddy, faithful and just. We had a relationship that lasted 17 years on the courses, much of it with success, in no small way due to Jack's skill as a golfing advisor, attendant and supporter. In countless ways, he was the perfect caddie, robust enough to carry the heaviest of bags, energetic enough to do the hard work of retrieving practice balls, ever confident and cheerful, with never a hint of criticism when his master was performing poorly. Jack was a handy golfer in his own right, which gave him an insight and sympathy for what his "bag" was going through. Like all the caddies of his era, and those who came before, Jack never bothered with distances of shots to be played, instead he knew exactly what club was needed, having computed the various factors that were pertinent. Not that he ever offered advices if he were not asked for them. He knew better than that. He was of the school that encouraged a player's self-reliance, and in that, a caddie was a supporter and not a managing director.

He became the Champion of the touring caddies of his time, protective of the lesser light. On one visit to Eire, he was missing from the first tee in the morning round. His friend Blondie, who use to caddie for Kel Nagle, took up my bag and said, 'Jackie will be a bit late today. He's got 'eld up', which was mystifying since he was ever punctual. I later learnt that he had been 'eld up by the Dublin Police after a stout and rough defence of poor little Mac (Dai Rees's caddie) during an attack by the local caddies who tried to drive the English out! Jack would have been lethal in a pub fight.

In all the 17 years of fun and games, I never appreciated his full character. It was only after he was struck down with his diabetes, that I came to see what I had missed. Blinded and bed-ridden, with every reason to hate his life and resent his cruel fate, he was the opposite. Exuding good humour and optimism he made me feel inadequate in my own puny efforts at dignity. Jack in his own way was a giant of a man, with much to pass on to his fellow human beings. As long as I live, I will think of him with affection and a little awe.'

Sometime after Alf's death, son John took the following phone call from Judy, the landlady of Alf's local, the Mason's Arms.

"John, I've been considering changing the pub's name to *The Alfie Fyles*, which I thought would be a fitting tribute to him, but they have dug their heels in and won't let me make the change. I'm gutted, but what I am doing is calling the front lounge after him, if that's Ok with you."

Naturally John and the rest of the family agreed and it was assumed that the locals would enjoy Alf's notoriety for years to come. What no one realised was that the news would spread worldwide. A few years ago, a party of Americans were playing at Royal Birkdale. Knowing of Alfie and having heard that the name of the Mason's Arms had been changed, they asked in earnest if anyone knew where they could find 'The Alfie Fyles.' They were then told the full story, after which they spent some time raising a glass to the four in the 'Alfie Fyles Lounge' instead.

On 15th December 2005, Teddy Halsall died aged 66, following a short illness, and on July 7th 2007 Albert died aged 70. After his death, The Park Golf Club wanted to commemorate the four caddies by naming a different hole after each of them. However, the local council put pressure on them and said they could have only three holes. The first one is now named Leigh Way, the eighth is called Halsall's, and the fifteenth they called Fyleses.

So ended an era. Many newspaper and internet articles have been written about our Birkdale Boys and their 'winnings', and people still talk fondly of Alf and his colleagues, and how Alfie's yardages in particular proved a godsend for each of his 'bags' that saved many a ball from ending in the rough.

Printed by: Copytech (UK) Limited trading as Printondemand-worldwide,
9 Culley Court, Bakewell Road, Orton Southgate,
Peterborough, PE2 6XD